PRAISE FOR *THE FUTURE HOME IN THE 5G ERA*

'This book takes an in-depth look at one of the most fascinating challenges of today: It sheds light on the emergence of a radical new experience of home driven by new technologies such as 5G, AI, eSIM and edge computing. And by using a powerful mix of real-life examples, strategic frameworks and thought-leading themes, it brings some great new insights for business leaders in the ecosystem connected to the Future Home. A must-read.'
Vinod Kumar, CEO, Vodafone Business

'As new technologies such as 5G and others disrupt our daily life – including our homes – this book shines new light on how communications service providers can thrive and grow in a landscape full of opportunities but also full of competitors pushing from many sides. It is an inspiring roadmap for leaders to do the right strategic steps into the promising era of the Future Home.'
Mari-Noëlle Jégo-Laveissière, Deputy CEO/Chief Technology and Innovation Officer, Orange Group

'An inspiring book that helps industry leaders to finally capture the opportunity of the fast-growing Future Home market. The authors provide great insights about the impediments and challenges of the Future Home market as well as a practical guide on how to resolve them.'
Dr Dirk Wössner, Member of the Board of Management, Deutsche Telekom/Managing Director, Telekom Germany

'A comprehensive well-written book on the impact of new technologies such as 5G on the rapidly evolving Future Home. With a smart strategic framework complemented by compelling real-life examples and use cases, this book is an inspirational call-to-action.'
Eric Bruno, Senior Vice President of 5G, Content and Connected Home Products, Rogers Communications

'*The Future Home in the 5G Era* gives executives a language and a framework to determine how they will evolve their products, services and strategies to flourish and innovate in a large, fast growing market.'
Clive Selley, CEO, Openreach

'*The Future Home in the 5G Era* brings some great new insights into the new hyper-connected home environment in which devices and apps will work together seamlessly to respond and anticipate customers' needs. With grounded research and innovative ideas, this book makes a stringent case for business leaders in any sector relevant to the emerging Future Home market with its enormous new opportunities. A must-read.'
Babak Fouladi, Member of Board/Chief Technology and Digital Officer, KPN Group

'This is an inspiring book on how we can understand the emergence of a new experience of home and on how companies can seize the enormous business opportunities connected to this new experience. New perspectives, fresh concepts, unexpected ideas abound. *The Future Home in the 5G Era* is a ground-breaking book.'
Ben Verwaayen, ex CEO BT Group, Alcatel-Lucent

'Unfulfilled promise or future revolution – the connected home remained an enigma until the appearance of this analysis. The authors make a compelling case that cloud and 5G connectivity will ultimately deliver the seamless platform play the world is waiting for. And in delivering this message they sparkle with ideas and innovative concepts – small wonder, given their collective entrepreneurial, corporate, tech and multi-industry experience.'
Jens Schulte-Bockum, COO, MTN Group

'*The Future Home in the 5G Era* comes at an opportune time, as science and new digital technologies unleash disruptive change across all fronts, transforming the (digital) lives of almost every individual: as private person, as customer, as manager, as citizen or in other roles and function.
An inspiring book – with fascinating stories, well researched, clearly explained.'
Prof Dr-Ing Boris Otto, Managing Director, Fraunhofer ISST (Institute for Software and Systems Engineering)

'The nature and experience of home is fundamentally changing with 5G. Well researched and with concrete suggestions on 5G implementation, this valuable guide will help firms and leaders seize the opportunities of an emerging multi-billion-dollar market: The Future Home in the 5G era.'
Igor Leprince, Chair, WM5G Board

The Future Home in the 5G Era

Next generation strategies for
hyper-connected living

Jefferson Wang
George Nazi
Boris Maurer
Amol Phadke

KoganPage

Publisher's note

Every possible effort has been made to ensure that the information contained in this book is accurate at the time of going to press, and the publishers and authors cannot accept responsibility for any errors or omissions, however caused. No responsibility for loss or damage occasioned to any person acting, or refraining from action, as a result of the material in this publication can be accepted by the editor, the publisher or the authors.

First published in Great Britain and the United States in 2020 by Kogan Page Limited

2nd Floor, 45 Gee Street
London
EC1V 3RS
United Kingdom

122 W 27th St, 10th Floor
New York, NY 10001
USA

4737/23 Ansari Road
Daryaganj
New Delhi 110002
India

www.koganpage.com

Kogan Page books are printed on papers from sustainable forests.

ISBN   978 1 78966 552 9
Ebook   978 1 78966 557 4

British Library Cataloguing-in-Publication Data

A CIP record for this book is available from the British Library.

Library of Congress Cataloging-in-Publication Data

LCCN: 2020000244

Typeset by Integra Software Services, Pondicherry
Print production managed by Jellyfish
Printed and bound by CPI Group (UK) Ltd, Croydon, CR0 4YY

CONTENTS

ABOUT THE AUTHORS

Jefferson Wang is a Managing Director with Accenture Strategy in their Communications, Media and Technology practice and leads the Communications Industry globally for Accenture Strategy. For two decades, he has focused on the wireless industry, working with network operators, device manufacturers, technology platform providers, content developers and start-ups through the end-to-end product development lifecycle.

Jefferson also leads Accenture's 5G global initiatives for the post-smartphone era, developing strategies and use cases to monetize 5G deployments. His client work takes place at the intersection of strategy, business and technology – converging the Future Home, autonomous vehicles and smart cities ecosystems.

Jefferson has appeared on CNN and Mobile World Live TV, is a regular speaker at Mobile World Congress and his perspectives have been featured in the *Wall Street Journal, USA Today, Fortune*, the *New York Times*, the *Washington Post, WIRED* and others.

Jefferson is a serial entrepreneur. Prior to Accenture he was a Senior Partner who led a broadband, wireless and media start-up to a successful exit. He holds a bachelor's degree in Mechanical Engineering from the University of Maryland, College Park. He is based in San Francisco.

George Nazi is a Senior Managing Director at Accenture, leading their Communications and Media Industry practice globally. He is a recognized technology leader known for blending strategic vision and operational execution, bringing a unique blend of executive acumen, global team building, and more than 25 years of industry experience transforming large organizations and operations.

Prior to joining Accenture, George served as President and Executive Vice President of Global Customer Delivery at Alcatel-Lucent, managing a workforce of more than 40,000. As President of Networks and IT infrastructure at BT (British Telecom), his most significant achievement was his leadership of the '21st Century Network' (21CN) transformation programme for BT, remaking the portfolio, enhancing the customer experience and building the next generation Network and OSS/BSS. He also served as Global Services CTO and Global VP of Networks, responsible for the design and deployment of BT's Global IP/MPLS network across 170 countries. George regularly authors whitepapers and articles on digital innovation and growth in the communications and media industry.

George holds bachelor's and master's degrees in Electrical Engineering and Computer Science from Tulsa University. George is based in Brussels.

Boris Maurer is a Managing Director with Accenture Strategy leading their Communications, Media and Technology practice in Europe. He also leads Digital Transformation for the Accenture Communications, Media and Technology industries globally. He has served telecommunications, energy and high-tech clients for more than two decades and has helped clients develop strategies for connected home and living spaces.

Boris has deep expertise in large-scale transformations, innovation, product development, governance, digital ecosystem plays and go-to-market strategies. He is an experienced entrepreneur with a focus in the IoT and artificial intelligence space and has founded and/or co-led several start-ups including WinLocal, yetu, smartB and connctd.

Boris has also worked in the public sector including the German Chancellery, and has helped regional governments, ministries and public institutions. He has written several books and articles about growth, innovation and how to win in times of disruptive change.

Boris holds a master's degree in Economics from the University of Bonn and a PhD in Economics from the University of Mannheim and the Institut d'Economie Industrielle (IDEI) in Toulouse. Boris is based in Berlin.

Amol Phadke is a Managing Director at Accenture in their Communications, Media and Technology business and leads the Accenture Network Services practice globally, driving the network services portfolio and helping CXO clients in all areas of digital network transformation, network economics and strategy, 5G, SDN/NFV, cloud, new OSS systems, next-generation operations and connected home solutions. He also sits on the Governing Board of Linux Foundation Networking (LFN).

Based in London, Amol is a recognized industry leader with more than 20 years of international industry experience providing technology and business leadership in networked IT, internet and telecoms, including strategy definition, driving large scale engineering development and delivery units and leading global multi-discipline teams. He has authored several whitepapers and articles on network transformation including 5G, software-defined networking and AI-powered operations. Prior to joining Accenture, Amol served as Senior Director for Alcatel-Lucent's Asia-Pacific network professional services business and worked at BT (British Telecom) as Chief Architect for their IP & Data global '21st Century Network' (21CN) platforms.

Amol holds a master's degree in Telecommunications Engineering from the University of Southern California, and a double degree executive MBA from UCLA, California-National University of Singapore (NUS). He was awarded the C H Wee Gold Medal for outstanding academic achievement in the executive MBA programme.

ACKNOWLEDGEMENTS

This book is about an idea – the Future Home. An idea that has yet to materialize, though it certainly will soon given the advancements in technologies that will enable it. This expectation has set a vast range of experts around the world thinking and strategizing about how the Future Home concept could play out, both technologically and in terms of business and marketing to consumers. To best advise businesses on working in this area, we therefore cast our net wide in seeking out inputs to our book.

That started with our author team. We come from different backgrounds with different perspectives. Some of us look at the Future Home through the lens of technology, others analyse it from the point of view of business strategy. That we were eventually able to strike the right balance was down to extensive consultation with industry strategists, technologists and aspiring entrepreneurs, among them many long-standing clients. Their inputs, collected from different geographies and areas of industry, have been critical in shaping our analyses, observations and conclusions. To all of them, we would like to express a huge thank you. Their support was instrumental in making this book happen.

Among the many valuable exchanges we had, the discussions with Dave Raggett, who leads the World Wide Web Consortium (W3C) Web of Things working group, and Nik Willetts, CEO of TM Forum, helped us shape our views on how to foster collaboration and standardization in the telecommunications industry. Glenn Couper, Jeff Howard, Kevin Petersen and Barbara Roden of AT&T provided valuable insight around enabling technologies in the consumer market. Lise Fuhr and Alessandro Gropelli, CEO and Director of the European Telecommunications Network Operators Association (ETNO) respectively, informed our strategic thinking. The views of Axel Schüßler, co-founder of connctd, and Jacob Fahrenkrug, CTO at yetu, helped us form a robust stance on privacy, security and interoperability. The knowledgeable perspectives of

Christine Knackfuß from Deutsche Telekom and Christian von Reventlow from Telstra on creating a framework for IoT in Europe enriched our analysis of trust, experience and scalability for platform models in the communication service provider sector. Professor Helle Wentzer from Aalborg University sharpened our view on healthcare in the Future Home. Junko Hiraishi, Masao Kubo, Koichi Moriyama, Shoichi Nakata, Yoji Osako, Yusuke 'Luke' Saito, Yuya 'Rex' Tanaka and Atsuro Wakazono of Docomo guided us expertly on the trajectories the development of new products for the Future Home might take.

We also wish to thank a range of Accenture colleagues who directly contributed to making this book a reality. Greg Douglass, Mark Knickrehm, Michael Lyman and Andy Walker skillfully supported us on business and technology strategies for this new Future Home market. Rajeev Butani, Saleem Janmohamed, Silvio Mani, Andy McGowan, Gene Reznik, Youssef Tuma, Francesco Venturini and John Walsh gave us their valuable insights and guidance on industry and Future Home trends. Furthermore, Afzaal Akhtar, Christian Hoffmann, Dr Imran Shah and Robert Wickel provided the team with guidance on the Future Home and its economic potential, while Andrew Costello, Tejas Rao, Hillol Roy and Peters Suh contributed their inputs on the evolution of 5G business models and technologies. The expertise of Bryan Adamson, Samir Ahshrup, Mayank Bhatnagar, Kishan Bhula, Katharine Chu, Jorge Gomez, Aaron Heil, Kevin Kapich, Kevin Karjala, Muzaffar Khurram, Joel Morgenstern, Ram Natarajan, Alexandra Sippin Rau, Eduardo Suarez and Kevin Wang also contributed to our thinking around 5G. Thanks are also due to teams from the Accenture Dock, Accenture Research and Fjord, part of Accenture Interactive, who were involved in creating 'Putting the Human First in the Future Home'[1], an inspiring research report compiled by Paul Barbagallo, Claire Carroll, Rachel Earley, David Light, Laurence Mackin and Iana Vassileva.

Putting so much expert thought and inspiration between two book covers while keeping it accessible to general business readers was an achievement attributable in large part to the marketing team at Accenture. We are grateful to Karen Wolf, Rhian Pamphilon and Sonya Domanski. And we greatly benefitted from the content development, publishing, writing and editing experience of Jens Schadendorf, Titus Kroder and John Moseley.

Also thank you to Tom, Winnie, Ethan, Julia and Connor Polen for opening their home to ethnographic field research to better define the Future Home. And to Katie Peterson, Laura Recht and Sara Reich from the Accenture Strategy offering development team and to Mark Flynn and his Accenture Research team.

And finally, we'd like to thank Chris Cudmore, Susi Lowndes, Natasha Tulett, Vanessa Rueda, Nancy Wallace and Helen Kogan from Kogan Page, the publisher of this book, for the enduring commitment to and trust in our project.

Above all, though, we wish to thank all our families and friends for their support and encouragement.

Jefferson: A big thank you goes to my mother Susan Sumei Chang Wang and to my late father Paul Mingteh Wang, who encouraged me to try everything, helped me connect different perspectives, allowed me to find my passions, but only forced me to learn one thing – perseverance. I also would like to thank my wife Bess and son Jefferson Paul for their unconditional support, turning confusion into clarity and making each day a masterpiece. And I am grateful to Dr Matt Supple, who always pushed me to find creative solutions in leadership, held me accountable to humble me and inspired me to help tomorrow's leaders today.

George: I want to say thank you to Becca, my wife, my children Lia, Catarina and Daniel, as well as to my extended family: my mother Ninawa, my late father Abboud, and my brothers and sisters Fadi, Nada, Camille and Amal who raised me and supported me throughout my career. You all provided input to this book too, for which I am grateful.

Boris: Patience, support as well as open and candid critique are key ingredients of such a project, as for any professional career. My wife Lucinde as well as my daughters Hannah and Katharina gave that in abundance, for which I thank them.

Amol: I would like to thank my amazing wife Sonal and my daughter Arya for being the constant source of inspiration and support that has immensely helped all my work. I am also eternally grateful to my parents Uday and Saroj for being the bedrock that has made all of this possible.

Introduction

The Future Home in the 5G era and beyond

Home is where the heart is, so the saying goes. The old adage conveys a powerful truth that is increasingly relevant in the era of digital transformation. Because in essence it assumes that 'at home' can be anywhere. As long as emotional roots anchor us in a specific place or environment, the exact physical location of 'at home' becomes irrelevant.

In the era of advanced technologies, feeling at home depends mainly on the quality of the user experiences provided by the digital services that surround us, whether we're stationary or mobile. If, for example, such services become so seamless and ubiquitous that we can start watching a film on a screen in our living room, then continue without interruption or hassle on the screens of the autonomous vehicle we boarded to get to a dinner with friends, we are likely to feel 'at home' regardless of whether we are between four walls or on four wheels.

In this book we assume that the traditional notion of home as a static shelter will soon be entirely replaced by the new consumer mindset of 'at home is everywhere'. Central to this will be the idea that anything that means home to us – from our favourite room temperature and air quality to our preferred light shades, entertainment and education suites, fitness and health devices, door security features and refrigerator contents – will very soon be emulated in outstanding quality via advanced, seamless and intelligent technology wherever we go: in an autonomous vehicle, at a holiday resort, on a leisure cruise, or even, with allowances for the needs of others, during a stopover at our in-laws. This means, in essence, that our home will turn into an envelope wrapped around us throughout the day.

Consider the point connectivity has already arrived at today. We seem to be approaching the age of hyper-connectivity full-throttle. The broad digital transformation of society means that wave after wave of connectivity technology is turning the world of ordinary objects into one of connected intelligent items – the frequently invoked Internet of Everything. The benefits for our social life are massive. Mobile and digital technology already enables us to stay in touch over enormous distances. It allows us to monitor the moments, moods and well-being of people far away, and we can co-work and even participate in a romantic relationship from almost anywhere in the world. What meant 'home' to us for centuries has already started to morph into a fluid hyper-connected lifestyle filled with highly personalized services based on new technologies.

The Future Home: The hub for hyper-connected living

To frame this thrilling, emerging world, we've coined the term Future Home, which also gives us the title of this book. We see the meaning of this phrase as very specific, exclusively reserved for the home that finally and truly delivers on the promise of seamless, highest-quality and genuinely life-enhancing digital services.

What is it that makes us think the Future Home is within sight? It is the growing number of enabling technologies maturing to a level of quality that will allow them to render the home intelligent, aware, able to understand, anticipate, predict and decide or provide relevant options. The main plank among these new technologies is the 5G wireless radio standard and its possible advantages: near-real-time responsiveness (ultra-reliable low-latency), very fast speeds (enhanced mobile broadband), connecting almost all devices (massive Internet of Things or IoT) and network slicing. This is, in our view, going to be the number one Future Home driver among all the novel enabling technologies. However, artificial intelligence (AI), edge computing and advanced data analytics are similarly important as they will enable the outstanding user experience we envisage. Enabled by 5G connectivity, they will reach the height of their potential in the Future Home.

As a feeling of 'at home' will always be relevant to human beings, those technologies will turn the Future Home into the central enabling hub of densely digitalized lifestyles for people from all walks of life. In such hyper-connected homes, we will have remote doctor's appointments, learn with holograms of teachers and students, and have access to services via any surface or display at hand. Advanced home tech will also think ahead for us, doing things like checking for unexpected road construction to ensure you arrive on time at that important work meeting. Days in advance, intelligent kitchens will have thought about your birthday party, asked the invited friends for dietary restrictions and, in response to their replies, stocked up automatically on just the right amount of personalized food based on preferences.

Roadmaps and capabilities for success in the new home market

In this radical perspective on Future Home life, our book lays out practical business strategies that allow a wide spectrum of sectors along the value chain of home services to make the most of the newly emerging markets. Among many other things, we show business practitioners the obstacles that need to be overcome so that we can create the Future Home. But we also crucially introduce readers to roadmaps and core capabilities that make them best placed to turn the opportunities of these new markets into value and profit.

We open our analysis of the Future Home with a brief scenic immersion in the day of a 'person on the street'. This character, described in Chapter 1, is supported by digital services constantly. Following such an individual through the day colourfully illustrates our view that the Future Home will be the main enabling hub for hyper-connected life regardless of its dwellers' physical locations.

Then we flip our perspective. From one possible lifestyle we enlarge the picture to describe a comprehensive typology of Future Home dwellers and how their lives will look when assisted by advanced home tech. The second chapter is therefore entirely dedicated to modern socio-demographic trends as well as the attitudes and mindsets of Future Home users – families, singles, youngsters and seniors from many contexts. Readers will realize one important imperative here: businesses interested in entering the Future Home market must focus on human needs, desires and dreams first and then create the technology stacks that fit these human requirements. Up to now, promising technologies have all too often been solutions in search of a human problem – thus failing to spark mass user demand. One of the central tenets of this book is to stick to a strict human-centric stance instead of imposing the marvels of new technologies on people regardless of need or desire.

In Chapter 3 we look at two of the mindsets from Chapter 2 in more detail, one giving us a window into family life and the other an overview of advanced healthcare at home. This provides a clear picture of how Future Home technology will need to be able to not only respond intelligently to the needs of different home users, but also communicate with service providers from outside the home and even with other Future Homes.

Experience-rich home services: Still held back by low tech

User experiences in today's connected homes – we eschew the term 'smart homes', as it's undeserved – are still basic. As we lay out in the fourth chapter, they fall utterly short of an 'at home everywhere' experience. Worse, their sluggish primitivism seems to be caused by a chicken or egg problem: without enough high-quality and experience-rich consumer services, there will be no appetite for more advanced home technology, but without demand, the business cases that could drive Future Home development will not be created.

Technologically, today's connected homes are held back by too many isolated point-to-point device solutions without overarching orchestration.

They're a hassle to set up, in other words, and don't deliver the seamless interconnectivity and interoperability that could genuinely assist us, as in the example of the birthday party, in which the kitchen, calendar, ecommerce and address book work as one. This disjointedness, in particular, gives the tech a bad name and impedes expansion of demand. For the Future Home market to take off, much more service quality and tech orchestration is needed.

Beyond the problems of fragmentation and inadequate device orchestration, we also show how the arrival of the Future Home is held back by issues such as the high cost of connected devices and the shortcomings of the connectivity fragmentation in the home today with Wi-Fi, ZigBee, Z-Wave, Bluetooth and other standards. And we show how the incoming 5G wireless standard will change things, acting as a powerful consolidator and a kick-starter for highly commercial Future Home markets.

Data security: The factor putting communications service providers (CSPs) in pole position

Nowhere do we interact with technology more intimately than at home. Therefore, data privacy and data security, as well as ethical standards on what tech-born intelligence is allowed to decide, will nowhere be as paramount as in the Future Home. We devote the whole of Chapter 5 to this important subject, a leading theme of our time and one of the most decisive factors for the emergence of the Future Home market. Just a few breaches, leaks, hacks or other data failures can obviously have enormously detrimental effects on user trust and willingness to accept advanced tech. Data security and data privacy, as well as ethically acting machine intelligence, are therefore make-or-break criteria for the success of the Future Home as a business case.

We postulate that users should be given absolute sovereignty over their data and that communications service providers (CSPs), platform providers, device manufacturers, cloud providers and third parties involved in Future Home ecosystems should work towards high and universal security standards to reinforce home tech against bad actors.

With regard to consumer trust, we make the point that CSPs such as wireless network operators, incumbent telephone operators or cable network businesses are well placed to inspire such faith, being the only parties with experience of handling sensitive user data in huge quantities for decades without significant breaches. What's more, they will be the players phasing in 5G networks, so will control one of the main Future Home enabling technologies.

Orchestrating data management as a consumer trustee: The holy grail

But which actors are best placed to be the orchestrating hand so badly needed in today's technologically incoherent homes? Our answer, condensed in Chapter 6, is, again, CSPs. No other businesses have such a high trust track record, millions of relationships with end-users, and long-term experience of running critical communications infrastructure.

But in the era of the Future Home, even CSPs cannot go on catering for their customers the old way. They need a radical revamp to become more agile, innovative and responsive to customers. Otherwise, we argue, they will not be able to conquer the economically attractive position of orchestrator for user services and data to improve lives. Without deep-running operative reform, many of them will lose out to other more platform-style parties taking that privileged role. We show what's needed for such thoroughgoing reform.

Overcoming inertia, tech hurdles and entrenched attitudes

What is also clear is that the Future Home will be built around data – massive amounts of it – and pervasive information flows in the home. Therefore, businesses involved in home tech must open up and either form or join home tech platforms. Only a platform nourishes itself by amassing user information to levels that can be transformed into insights and these, in the end, are what will feed experience-rich home services.

For CSPs, a group of companies given special focus in this book, this question will probably become one of survival. Historically accustomed to deliver hardware and connectivity in the shape of vertical organizations with siloed departments, most of them are still far from prepared to be the primary managers and traffic wardens of data flows in the Future Home. Just controlling data infrastructure, as they have done for decades in their traditional role, will not suffice here. We look in detail at the nature of their new role as Future Home orchestrators in Chapter 7.

Overall, the siloed containment of usage data by proprietary home device makers has been a huge problem. Up to now, it has hindered the creation of experience-rich home services as it prevents devices from sharing the information necessary not only to provide seamless services collaboratively, but also for the home as a whole to learn and develop its offering intelligently in line with changing user needs. We are not yet there by any means, but we hope that the multi-billion-dollar business opportunity the Future Home offers can act as argument enough to bring more coordination, interoperability and cooperation into this promising market. All industries involved, all partners joining ecosystems around Future Home markets, should open up to the idea of sharing standardized data for home solutions to improve the user experience.

In its last part, this book looks into ways to overcome the hurdles of old-style technologies and entrenched business attitudes. In Chapter 8, we dedicate much thought to strategies for CSPs and other ecosystem members on how to overcome data silence between Future Home devices and the different service, hardware and software providers involved. Here, we stress the necessity to create joint standardized data reservoirs that allied ecosystem partners must be able to tap into for good and experience-rich home services to improve the user experience.

Finally, to cap things off, in Chapter 9 the most important strategic points and pivots to keep in mind on the journey to success in the emerging

Future Home markets are summarized for quick, practical referencing by industry practitioners from all relevant sectors.

This book is, beyond the CSP sector, equally relevant to all other players within Future Home ecosystems: device manufacturers, platform providers, app designers and the industrial players that will provide goods and services to the inhabitants of Future Homes, such as retailers and healthcare or entertainment providers.

Essentially, the message for any relevant business is: as unpromising as the connected home market might look today, this is about to change – drastically. 5G is going to create a vast new world of opportunity in the Future Home, but also a great risk of leaving many behind.

This book will show you how to capitalize on the former and avoid the latter.

Commensurate with the importance and currency of this topic, there is significant movement in the market. As we went to press, one example is the establishment of Project Connected Home over IP (https://www.connectedhomeip.com), a working group for a new connectivity standard to increase compatibility among Future Home products. The authors regularly comment on new developments. Highlights of that commentary can be viewed at www.accenture.com/FutureHome.

1

A day in the life of a Future Home

CHAPTER SUMMARY

The Future Home, the concept this book is built around, is a radical departure from today's standards of digital sophistication in homes. In just a few years people will be living lifestyles that are intensely assisted by intelligent digital technology. For them, 'home' will be everywhere. Technology will be their permanent companion and great enabler in everything, from meal preparation to childminding to working remotely. This will be a world unlike any seen previously, so before we begin to analyse its workings in detail, we should take some time simply to look at it. In this chapter, therefore, we present a sneak preview of the Future Home in the 5G era.

In a northern hemisphere mega city, it is Tuesday, 6.30 am – roughly half an hour before John A Centure, a 41-year-old senior underwriter for a global insurance company, typically gets up. John is single. His digital bedroom command node has already batted away the first tasks of the day and now makes the solar-powered curtains glide open. The room's recessed lights, matching the exact daylight spectrum outside at any minute, turn on gradually. Gentle music starts to play at a very low volume, the beats matching John's heart rate and gradually increasing. Minute by minute the man in his sensorized high-tech pyjamas is drawn from deep sleep to a drowsy smile at the sunlight that is by now flooding the bedroom.

Fed by data from the bed, pyjamas and a wearable device, the bedroom node has calculated John's ideal wake-up time. In calculating this, it balanced a maximum of rapid eye movement (REM) sleep, the most relaxing human sleep phase, with news it had just received from the mobility node of the apartment's Future Home system: the autonomous bus John usually takes to work is out of action today.

A life with the problems taken care of

This is just one of many decisions the Future Home will make for its inhabitant. To be on the safe side, it woke John up about 30 minutes earlier and added extra time for an alternative journey to work: a short walk to the municipal rail station followed by a four-stop ride to the Balboa Park stop. As John gets out of bed and glances out of the window, the Future Home central command node automatically brings up today's weather, his calendar and his new commute, overlaid using augmented reality on the glass window. It follows a visualization of the walk to the rail station. John accepts each decision because he knows he can rely on the system 100 per cent, allowing him to leave aside much of what concerns us today: no anxious speculating about different options, no hectic adjustments to unforeseen circumstances – the Future Home anticipates the problems, fixes the simple ones before they arise, and proactively provides relevant options for the more complex problems. That is what John has learned since moving in two years ago.

At home alone, and out with friends – simultaneously

It is now 7 am. Leaving home is still an hour away. Putting on his workout gear and his smart glasses, John joins a streamed virtual workout meet-up with two of his friends. They are in the same virtual gym, chatting with each other. To increase competition, each can see the other's scoreboard of calories burned right from their bedrooms. Each workout is tailored. As John is recovering from a sprained wrist, the physical activities node of his Future Home thinks it better for him to avoid push-ups and focus on his lower body instead. John is today's 'calorie champ' and the system has prepared a highlight reel of his workout session, set to his favourite music, presenting his score at the end. It asks John for permission to post the clip on social media platforms to a group of friends that all three have in common, which he gives by simply saying 'Yes.'

The ever-present personal assistant and servant

After the morning workout John enters the bathroom to brush his teeth. The Future Home system raises the air temperature a few degrees and turns on the shower at his desired water temperature. Weight sensors in the bathroom floor relay data to the bathroom node. John is still slightly behind his weight-loss goal so the node starts a discreet conversation with its opposite number in the kitchen where an algorithm asks John if he'd like to eliminate sugar from his morning coffee for the rest of the week. That should help him to arrive at the target weight. As John dries off, his intelligent closet picks two outfits based on the professional and private events on his calendar that day. While he decides on one of the two, an interactive assistant speaker integrated into each room reads out the morning news.

7.30 am – John enters the kitchen. A robotic arm has prepped and cooked him breakfast, balancing nutrient and caloric intakes to help lose the one last pound this week before his weekend beach vacation. His virtual personal assistant uses pattern matching technology, machine learning and natural language processing to provide the right information at the right time. It has studied his behaviour and is trained to know the right time to provide him with more information on the person he will see during his first meeting – a client who wants to take out an earthquake policy. Then, as he has just finished his first cup of coffee, sadly unsweetened, a hologram playback of his last meeting with this client, a month ago, is displayed in front of him. The meeting was volumetrically captured at John's office. Everyone opted into a privacy statement allowing a digital memory capture to replace meeting minutes.

The empty home doing its homework

Once the breakfast is finished, the kitchen transforms into a living room where furniture is repurposed and the room reconfigured. A wall lights up and John's digital assistant displays a household checklist scheduled for today. Point 1: an automated vacuum cleaner will clean the carpets before it becomes a mop and does the tiles. Point 2: John's plants will receive their daily watering but are also due for a monthly fertilizer treatment. Point 3: the laundry hamper is near capacity and the Future Home suggests using video analytics to determine the colour, fabric type and shape of the clothes to more accurately separate the laundry prior to washing, drying and folding. But the home also points out that energy usage is cheaper after 9 pm, so John decides to defer the service until then. Point 4: since it's the first day of spring, with a higher than normal pollen count, new allergy medication is ordered and will be delivered today to John's delivery lockbox. Point 5: before leaving the Future Home, John is reminded to take his daily vitamins and blood pressure medication, so that the health node can send a treatment adherence confirmation to John's doctor and his insurance company for a monthly discount incentive.

At home while on the move to work

At 8.15 am John closes the door behind him and the home security node activates. It automatically locks the door, sending the home into energy-saving mode. John walks down his street. His Future Home has calculated 10 minutes of walking, giving him ample time to catch a train at 8.30 am. As he walks, his favourite podcast and navigation route are streamed to the smart glasses John wears on the end of his nose. The augmented reality feature overlays the quickest route in real time onto the sidewalk ahead of him, guiding him to the rail station.

At the station, the smart glasses guide John straight to the correct track and even to a platform spot where a carriage with free seats will come to a stop. John enters the train, falls into a seat and the podcast continues. But today's edition is boring, so John pushes up his glasses, which darkens the lenses and turns them into an immersive virtual reality device shielding his eyes from most of his surroundings. He enters a digital replica of his living room and begins to play a streaming multiplayer video game on the large-screen TV hanging on the virtual wall. His friends from this morning's workout session are all also live in the game during their morning commutes in autonomous vehicles. While playing the video game, they alternate between communicating with each other and voting on which exercises they want to do tomorrow morning. All of a sudden, a tiny figure appears in the bottom left corner of the display, letting John know that the train will arrive at Balboa Park in two minutes. John lets the device slip down his nose which lightens the lenses and instantly turns them into his normal reading glasses again, with augmented reality features where necessary. He gets off the train and is guided to the office.

At work and feeling very much at home

Hot-desking is the norm in offices now. John's smart glasses guide him to today's work spot, an elegant 10-square-meter, fully transparent office. Not just the desk, but the office where underwriters like John work, can change every day. Employers minimize their costs by picking the most affordable office spaces rented out at dynamic rates.

Still, once John gets into an office space for the day, everything is already there – thanks to his Future Home system, which knows where he is and what he is doing once he has left his apartment. His work office turns instantly into his familiar workspace at home, displaying framed desk pictures of his late father and his dog, Beethoven. His computer system is also ready to go, with the files for the first client meeting opening as John puts his jacket on a hanger. He is not constrained, however, by physical monitors, a keyboard or a desk. Depending on the files he needs, virtual walls and glass panes fill with the relevant presentations and spreadsheets for comparison and recommendation. John uses only minimal hand gestures to close sheets and move presentations around.

The first meetings and calls go well and at noon, lunchtime rolls around. John's food is delivered with the usual balanced nutrition but a slightly increased lean protein intake since he walked an extra 10 minutes to the rail station this morning. His Future Home has taken care of it all. After a quick bite, John gets a notification from his dating profile. Someone who finds him compatible has requested a virtual coffee and John decides to accept. It's all arranged on his multipurpose smart glasses. The fact that he wears formal office attire is no problem. He takes part in the virtual coffee date as a volumetric twin and can choose to wear whatever he wants. He decides on a combo of beige chinos, sneakers and a fitted dark-blue shirt. After some lively exchanges, John and his date decide to meet up in person at a later date. Riding the excitement, John goes right back to work for the remainder of the day.

Collapsing distance to maintain contact

At 6.30 pm John winds down in his apartment. The sun is setting and he gets a video call from his mother. John again pushes his specs into virtual reality mode. His mother is feeling nostalgic, she says, since her husband passed away of stomach cancer 20 years ago to this day. She asks John to go for a virtual walk with her. She is in her home hundreds of miles away while John sits on his living room sofa, but via this hologram call, mother and son are both transported to the tree-lined suburban street of John's childhood. The street and surroundings are presented just as they looked when John's father passed away. As his mother shares stories about his father, John asks if they can watch one of his father's volumetric recorded memories. She agrees and they are both greeted by his father's hologram, a virtual and volumetric set of messages he recorded for them both before he passed away. This makes John reflect on the fact that tomorrow is not guaranteed for anyone, on how suddenly loved ones can be lost, and on how lucky he is to still be able to spend time like this with his mother even though he no longer lives nearby.

2

Consumer needs in a hyper-connected world

CHAPTER SUMMARY

....

As we have seen in our examination of one person's life in the Future Home, the concept of the 5G-driven Future Home is not led by technology but by human needs and desires that technology is increasingly able to meet. These new habits and preferences are variable, depending on life stage, family status or age. Laying out the various socio-demographic profiles of consumers in the age of digital transformation and hyper-connected lifestyles is therefore essential. In this chapter, we identify five mega-trends shaping future hyper-connected lifestyles, and also the eight different types of user mindsets we expect to find in this new world.

....

In the era of digital transformation, the word 'home' has become an emotionally loaded and widely interpreted term. Whatever the meaning ascribed to it, it keeps its overwhelmingly positive connotation of a personal and emotional hub for daily life. This is what invites us to think ahead radically, ultimately imagining this feeling of home being available to people almost anywhere, not just within the traditional physical boundaries of a habitation.

Five megatrends shaping hyper-connected lifestyles

To deepen our analysis of the notions, physical realities and technologies involved in the homes of the future, it is worth extracting five megatrends that will, in our view, very likely define the relationship between humans and these homes. From such a list, first ideas for use cases and business models around the 5G-enabled Future Home can be filtered. These will be further detailed later in this book.

One: The hyper-connection and hyper-personalization of daily life

This is where we start: day-to-day life is changing rapidly under the auspices of the wholesale digital transformation of society. Via quickly evolving technologies, humans are becoming hyper-connected to objects and other people. We have started to intimately connect to our vehicles, light bulbs, domestic appliances and even brain waves. The list of objects and digital counterparts is endless, our era one of ever more densely woven digital networks between humans and devices of all sorts. According to International Data Corporation (IDC), there will be 41.6 billion connected IoT devices generating 79.4 zettabytes (ZB) of data by 2025.[1]

This era of the 'Internet of Everything' is profoundly affecting the way we live in general and the way we organize work and leisure time. But while various areas of our existence – home life, healthcare, work and life on the move – become increasingly connected to us, they often tend not to be connected to one another. Technologically, such areas are currently evolving in isolation, meaning consumers can often feel swamped with a chaos of incoherent services. To properly interconnect and really deliver experience-rich, hyper-personalized living services, devices need

Figure 2.1   Interconnecting the connected services – with the user at the centre

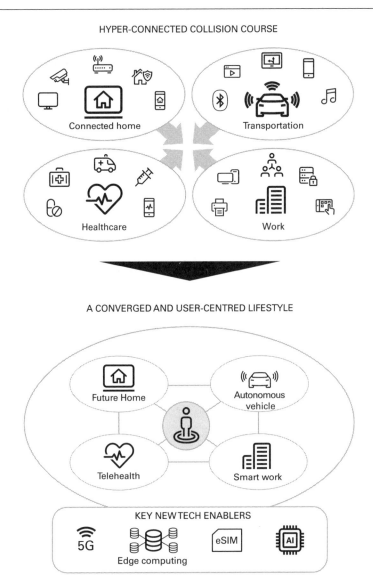

to be harmonized by technologies such as 5G, edge computing, eSIM and artificial intelligence (AI), which are still evolving and deploying.

With an increasingly hyper-connected lifestyle, humans move around a lot more than before. For work or leisure, we constantly change our location – between desks in rooms, between rooms in our homes and other buildings and between cities, regions, countries and continents. In doing so, we are often assisted by a small device such as a laptop, a smartphone, headphones and/or an intelligent watch – things many people might already be beginning to think of as a sort of home given the way such devices have grown to become their command centres for day-to-day life management.

The younger generations represent this trend the most with up to 35 days of vacation travel per year.[2] As a result, the notion of home has started to become blurry, no longer meaning only fixed walls and private space, but also dynamic and mobile environments for work and leisure that are strongly enabled by connected digital technology.

Two: Millennials and Gen Z, the principal architects of the Future Home

Megatrend number two is the emergence of generations with entirely new mindsets around user experience, spending habits and techno-logical preferences: Millennials, those born between 1980 and the mid-2000s, and the even younger Gen Z. Both generations will be-come, via their personal preferences, migration patterns, specific tech stacks and home service set-ups, the primary architects and builders of the Future Home.

In 2019 in the United States, the Millennial population of around 80 million overtook the Baby Boomers as the largest adult segment.[3] Globally, things are even more advanced: 1.4 billion Millennials walk the earth, becoming the most populous group at a global scale as far back as 1994.[4]

Beyond the head count, what are the socio-demographic characteris-tics of this age cohort? Crucially, Millennials and Gen Z overwhelmingly prefer to live in cities and will become the biggest spenders very soon. There are now 1,860 cities globally, each containing at least 300,000 inhabitants.[5] These are getting bigger, largely driven by the Millennials' urban-focused lifestyles. Today's 33 megacities of 10 million people or more will grow to a total of 43 megacities by 2030.[6]

More people per square metre creates the necessity for more agile and reliable coordination between them, and this trend is naturally building the case for more home technology to organize home lives. More people will be living in apartment blocks and smaller units and will therefore share more central services such as heating, water, electricity and connectivity networks. It is therefore important to find attractive home technology solutions not only for individual properties, but also for aggregate lives under one roof of an apartment block or even in city quarters. In many instances, Future Home technology will therefore inevitably overlap with some smart city technology.

What about the spending power of these new generations? In the US labour market, Millennials became the biggest segment back in 2016.[7] This trend is taking hold in many other countries. The World Data Lab therefore forecasts that Millennials' global spending power will have become greater than that of any other generation by 2020.[8] Inevitably then, this age cohort will shape and define technology use and business cases for the Future Home more than any other.[9]

A third feature marks out Millennials and Gen Z as defining forces of the Future Home. They are all digital natives, though to differing degrees. The youngest Millennials were children when the iPhone, the first mass-adopted smartphone, came to market in June 2007. So they strongly see home tech and services through a digital lens. Using virtual tours, for example, many purchase homes without having physically seen them – and then apply for mortgages on their phones rather than sitting down in person with a mortgage broker.[10]

The new generations are picky like none before when it comes to service quality. Accenture surveyed 26,000 consumers in 26 countries and found that of those who own or plan to purchase connected home services, 71 per cent would want to purchase connected home solutions from CSPs.[11] Furthermore, 55 per cent were planning to change their CSP[12] in the next year due to poor connectivity experience based on the current fixed-line architectures in their homes. This shows that CSPs must do a much better job of understanding the new generations to keep them on board.

The massive business opportunities of the Future Home, built to suit the demand profile of Millennials and Gen Z, will go way beyond connectivity into areas such as healthcare. In the Accenture survey, 49 per cent of respondents said they would choose their CSP for the delivery of home healthcare services.[13] Thirty per cent want virtual care, which could be administered in a Future Home environment, and interest in remote monitoring capabilities and video consulting is strong.[14] The younger generations are also much more likely to choose medical providers with strong digital capabilities, those who provide mobile or online access to test results (44 per cent of Millennials vs 29 per cent of Baby Boomers), electronic prescription renewals (42 per cent vs 30 per cent), and the ability to book, change or cancel appointments online (40 per cent vs 19 per cent). What is more, Millennials and Gen Z are especially inclined to drop today's primary care physicians and face-to-face consulting for non-traditional healthcare models such as remote medical consulting and treatment. Without a primary care physician, the new generations already seek novel types of routine medical services from retail clinics (41 per cent) and virtual care providers (39 per cent).[15]

That is by no means the end of the shifts these generations represent. They are, for example, much more likely to care about time outside work. A report conducted by the US White House[16] on the younger generation found that, compared to Generation X or the Baby Boomers, a greater proportion of this group valued life goals such as having time for recreation and finding new ways to experience things – in short, a better work–life balance. Much of that coveted leisure time is spent on experiencing and sharing on social media. Millennials and Gen Z are the first generations to be natives of Instagram, Facebook, YouTube, WeChat, Snapchat and other social media, with which they have largely grown up.

Millennials and Gen Z have fluid consumer expectations like no previous generation. Surveying 60 global retailers, Accenture found that nearly 40 per cent named the lack of loyalty among Millennials as their top concern.[17] Yet when we work to understand them more deeply, we find that Millennials and Gen Z can be loyal customers but only if they are treated well and pursued with personalized service offerings. They just want convenient ways to interact with their providers and brands, ideally through social media and messaging chats. That's as likely to be true for Future Home service providers of all types as it is for retailers.

Over the next 20 years or so, the home will therefore develop to become a hyper-connected hub of services that reaches way beyond traditional connected home services into advanced age and healthcare, social communications, community relations, purchasing, travel, childcare and work.

Three: The rapid ageing of society and the desire to age in place

Thanks to advances in education, quality of life and healthcare, the world is living longer. According to the United Nations World Population Prospects 2019, the global population over the age of 65 will increase from 9.3 per cent in 2020 to 15.9 per cent in 2050.[18] For perspective, there will be more than 727 million people over the age of 65 globally in 2020, equal to the third most populous country behind China and India. Even more staggering is the fact that by 2050, there will be more than 1.5 billion people over the age of 65 globally.

When you combine these facts with the already strained healthcare system, ageing in place is an attractive option for everyone involved. Ageing in place is defined as continuing to live and age in one's home or residence of choice for as long as possible. In a survey by the American Association of Retired Persons (AARP) in 2018, 76 per cent of advanced-aged people would like to remain in their current residence for as long as they can.[19]

The world will face major challenges to ensure that health and social systems are ready for this demographic shift. Health and well-being in advanced age supported by digital devices will be of exponential importance and will create a massively growing marketplace for service

Figure 2.2   The world is ageing[20]

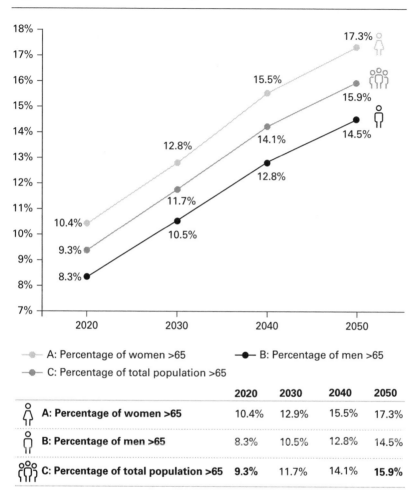

	2020	2030	2040	2050
A: Percentage of women >65	10.4%	12.9%	15.5%	17.3%
B: Percentage of men >65	8.3%	10.5%	12.8%	14.5%
C: Percentage of total population >65	9.3%	11.7%	14.1%	**15.9%**

providers of all kinds. This trend, like the other sociological mega currents we are defining, will also become a major driver for technological advancements in home technology. In line with the younger generations' preferences, as identified by our surveys, future healthcare will, to a large extent, take place at home. For ageing in place to be successful, we will need to bring the monitoring, peace of mind and healthcare services into the advanced-aged home, turning it into a Future Home. But this setting can do more than just enable telehealth or remote healthcare. The Future Home can help advanced-aged people stay connected with distant relatives, increase daily mental activity to strengthen connections between brain cells, and even help find ways for advanced-aged people to contribute back to society, helping them find renewed purpose.

Four: The rise of Do It For Me (DIFM) and the fall of Do It Yourself (DIY)

The digital services and technologies we enjoy such as voice assistants, apps, APIs, AI, sensors and mobile connectivity, to name but a few, are becoming better at anticipating our needs, making our experiences of digital services richer and more immediate. But as network speed, latency and density improve, the bar will be set ever higher. As a consequence, we are becoming pickier, more capricious and more fickle around services – especially when they are delivered in our home.

At the same time, a segment of consumers is shifting from a Do It Yourself (DIY) to a Do It For Me (DIFM) mindset. I let an autonomous robotic vacuum do it for me. I pay extra to furniture companies to deliver and assemble it for me. I subscribe to a meal service that delivers hot food to me. I use an app that finds people to walk my dog for me. A field experiment by the University of British Columbia and Harvard Business School found that people who spent $40 on time-saving conveniences were actually happier than when they spent $40 on material purchases.[21]

Still, our current connected homes are built for the DIY crowd, not the DIFM future. We spend 15 minutes watching a video on how to install a connected thermostat before spending another 30 to 60 minutes actually installing it. We have to spend time researching and reading fine print to determine if a new connected door lock we want to buy will integrate with our smart speaker, a decision we already made. We have to spend time downloading another app just to set up a connected light device only to have to re-enter the complex Wi-Fi password when the power goes out.

For the Future Home in 5G to gain mass adoption, the friction will have to be removed. The Future Home in 5G will work out of the box. These DIFM consumers will soon expect no less than seamless service implemented almost unnoticed. Home services will be perceived as 'just there', with no additional action required from the user: no assembly of parts and no complex identification procedures, but enormous expectations that home services can think ahead and pre-empt the need for users to specify the support they require. Of course there will always be a segment of consumers who are value-focused, a segment who want to learn by doing. But for the Future Home to successfully jump across the mass-adoption gap it will have to design for the DIFM segment first.

Five: 'Alone together' in the digitized habitat

Alone together. Oxymoron... or our new reality? Humans are fundamentally social and our relationships are based on good communication. But when you decompose communication down to its core, it is about you conveying a message and that message being received, heard and most importantly understood by someone else. So, in reality, humans are social but, more importantly, we all just simply want to be heard and understood.

The issue is that everyone has a story to tell but there aren't always trusted people available in front of you, trusted people who won't judge you while listening to your story, to receive, hear and understand that story. Technology has helped connect us to different groups of people virtually, but this means we aren't communicating and building relationships with those around us.

Technology, rather than catering to this elementary human disposition, tends to separate even people who live together, making them inclined to keep in remote contact with the outside world rather than paying attention to each other. How many times have you been in the same room with family or friends only to look up to see that everyone is focused on their screens? This is 'alone together' time. Simply because you are surrounded by people doesn't mean you cannot feel lonely if no one is talking or taking the time to focus and empathically listen. Technology may have connected us with others but it has replaced conversation with those in front of us. Unchecked, this could create an epidemic of loneliness.

Innovative use of user experience (UX) and service design in the Future Home to get technology to work against its own natural tendency would be an area of enormous social and economic value. Imagine a Future Home that is monitoring alone together time and finding ways to facilitate face-to-face conversations between family members or even help moderate in-person conflicts.

From a more general perspective, the next generation will also look back and judge the success of the Future Home by its ability to support and enhance our social lives instead of substituting them. As the conventional home of today, the Future Home will need to provide social meaning to its inhabitants. This will ultimately be rooted in the interaction with loved ones, friends and acquaintances as well as in running deep personal relationships – a major finding of our ongoing research about the home and how it is seen by residents.

How people really think and feel about homes – in eight mindsets

As we shift from today's technology-led DIY and fragmented connected home to tomorrow's DIFM Future Home focused on human-centred solutions, it's important to understand the challenges we need to overcome and capabilities we need to build to be prepared.

Accenture's Future Home concepts put the human at the heart. To do this, we leveraged Accenture research on the Future Home. In 2018, Fjord (a design and innovation consultancy, part of Accenture Interactive), Accenture Research and the Accenture Dock (Accenture's flagship multidisciplinary research and incubation hub) surveyed over 6,000 global participants across 13 geographies (United States, Brazil, United Kingdom, Sweden, Denmark, France, Germany, Italy, Spain, China, India, Japan and Australia).[22] The goal was to understand what people value at home, what new human behaviour patterns can be identified in the current connected home reality and how the changing relationship people have with the word 'home' can be better appreciated.

From this research, a clear segmentation of attitudes towards homes and technology was identified.[23] Understanding these categories is key in helping us appreciate how needs vary from person to person and what trajectories these different needs are likely to take in the future, allowing companies to tailor and target their offerings for Future Home markets with precision.

Figure 2.3   Four attitudes towards homes and technology

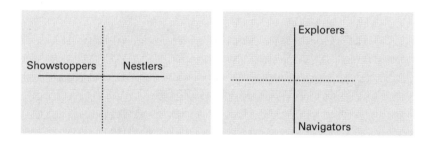

From our research, a spectrum of attitudes to a home emerges on an x-axis. At one end of the scale are the 'Showstoppers' who see their home as a passionate reflection of their personal brand and have designed spaces that excite them and impress guests. At the other end are the more level-headed 'Nestler' types whose priority is to create a sense of comfort, functional cosiness and safety for their family.

Offsetting this spectrum, we found another vertical axis based on technological awareness and preparedness for tech adoption. At the top of this new spectrum are the 'Explorers', the early adopters of products and services, proud to always use the latest tech. At the other are the tentative 'Navigators' who will only pick up new technology and find value in it once they have seen it succeed with others.

In the spaces defined by the intersection of these two axes, we found eight distinct mindsets. These mindsets represented different attitudes and human behaviours with regard to a home. The research further organized these mindsets into two major life stages: *with children* and *without children*.

In the next chapter, we'll take a much more detailed look at a couple of these types, but for now, let's get a general overview of all of them. We start with four mindsets for people with children.

Figure 2.4   Four mindsets for people with children[24]

Mindset 1: Drone Parents

Drone Parents are family types weighted heavily towards having a Showstopper home that makes people say 'wow' and are Explorers who early-adopt technology. The title refers to the fact that these are parents who value control, efficiency, convenience and privacy, and clearly see the advantage of using technology to provide an easier life and a safer Future Home for family. Drone Parents are prone to be alone together. Again, 'alone together' is the behaviour you may observe at a restaurant where a family is sitting together but each parent and child is absorbed in their own individual digital device, obviating any shared interests, activities and communication paths.

A typical Drone Parent's tech stack mainly aims at making the home more controllable, safe, functional and private. They order food and groceries for home delivery, use smart speakers, and control home and family remotely. What would make their life better is any technology or solution that is easy to install, manages kids' screen time, solves the 'alone together' issue and enables privacy.

Mindset 2: Hip-happening Parents

Hip-happening Parents, in contrast to Drone Parents, are pragmatic Nestlers, natural socializers and easy-going connectors. But similarly to Drone Parents, Hip-happening Parents share the Explorer or lead user view on technology. They see the fun side of tech. They want a creative and fashionable ambience that is seamlessly part of their lifestyle and they value everything that makes their home hipper. They want the convenience of DIFM but they do also want to feel safe if someone else is installing tech in their home.

Hip-happening Parents want their innovative and sociable home to allow good communication with family and provide the ability to relax without worry – to be able to kick back and enjoy a craft brew beer or kombucha in a wine glass, especially when the kids are occupied. Tech is important if it makes their day-to-day life more self-indulgent. They stream online content and entertainment shows throughout the home.

What would make their life better is tech-enabled, adaptable, fun spaces in the home that push the boundaries of physical walls, screen time monitors for kids and a seamless user experience of all digital devices in the home.

Mindset 3: Savvy Seniors

Similar to Drone Parents who love to make their home a show-stopping centrepiece of conversation, Savvy Seniors enjoy treating their home as a reflection of their own personal brand, a brand that they have worked very hard to build up over the years. However, they differentiate from Drone Parents in that they are Navigators with new technology. This advanced age group has a primary goal of displaying well-oiled tech assistance in their upmarket homes, but they are very careful not to be overly dependent on technology. They like technology that is both functional and luxurious.

It's important to Savvy Seniors that their home is impressive, upscale, and inspirational. It must offer them the opportunity to step back and marvel at their life's achievements.

At the same time, they need to feel safe, and they constantly worry about control and maintaining a balance between being always connected and enjoying life. They use technology for home safety, for monitoring their health and to boost their well-being. They deeply value good communication with family outside the home, especially grandchildren.

Their life could be improved by a better balance with technology dependence and even more sophisticated health tech that will likely become common in the Future Home, making trips to the doctor and hospital less necessary.

Mindset 4: Social Grandparents

The Social Grandparent is an advanced-aged single grandparent. She or he is a Navigator type when it comes to technology and a Nestler. Social Grandparents need to feel safe and comfortable and they see technology from a sober, functional angle, once it's been proven by someone they trust. Despite their advanced age, they are still busy people who use tech for keeping the home familiar, for connecting with friends and relatives and for staying in touch with the outside world.

Social Grandparents are often alone at home and they worry about control and independent living; ageing in place is very important. They want to feel secure – by being connected to others, having attentive neighbours that check in and perhaps by keeping a dog. They allow younger relatives to monitor them via remote cameras and sensors so they can live in their home as long as possible. They use health monitoring devices and look after their personal well-being. They listen to podcasts and use tech and social media to stay up to date and connected.

Life could be improved by helping them create more time to stay even better connected, by finding solutions to control unwanted advertising that interferes with social media or solutions to automate everyday home chores such as vacuuming the carpets and mopping the floor, which coincidentally also gets in the way of staying connected via social media.

Let's now look at the four mindsets for people *without* children.

Figure 2.5   Four mindsets for people without children[25]

Mindset 5: Ambience Leaders

Ambience Leaders want anyone who comes into their Showstopper home to realize it has been designed to impress. They are also Explorers of technology who pride themselves on buying and using the latest technology before others. They want hyper-connectivity, hyper-personalization and interconnection of the separate ecosystems in their lives such as home, transportation, health and work. Open and inviting, they crave an inspiring, aesthetically pleasing home, offering enriching sensory experiences, and likewise cherish tech that aids pleasure and well-being, things for which they will carve out significant portions of time. For example, they use smart ambient lighting to try to improve sleep patterns, and stay healthy using personal monitoring devices and apps. Life could be made even better for them with more new and immersive technology to help them visualize dreams and make them a reality.

Mindset 6: Wired-up Urbanites

The Wired-up Urbanite is a strong Explorer type, geared towards trying a new technology, with a Nestler attitude towards their home. Busy and active in their jobs and outside, they appreciate tech for everyday convenience and for keeping connected. They want to feel at their best in their home. Comfort is important to them, which means high-quality, well-designed products and services that just work.

The Wired-up Urbanite devours health and fitness solutions, especially if technology can bring health and fitness into their home for greater convenience. They want their homes to be serene, clean and stylish, dotted with quality luxury products, including those that enhance well-being. They want DIFM installation so that things are hidden and clean. What would improve their home life is even more tech that gives them empowering access to home services and high-quality products.

Mindset 7: Conscientious Controllers

Conscientious Controllers are Navigators, tending to lag slightly tech-wise, but are Showstoppers in the sense that they are self-assured, tidy and keep their home very organized for efficiency and maximum self-improvement. They want to inhabit homes that are tailored to health and lifestyle needs, as well as being clean, organized, efficient and offering each user the control of their mind, body and environment. These types already use voice assistants to get things done at home, as well as health and fitness apps and any tech stack that makes working at home flexible. The Conscientious Controller often has a home office where they can leave things and not worry about anyone else moving them. Seamless tech integration, sleep and well-being support, and ways that technology can think for them to help balance work and leisure would help them further.

Mindset 8: Chaotic Creatives

Finally, we arrive at the Chaotic Creatives. Navigators when it comes to tech and Nestlers with regards to creating a warm, comfortable home, these types tend to be private and disorganized. They use tech for convenience but are generally reluctant to invest in it. Chaotic Creatives get lost in their activities and often forget to organize and clean their homes until there is a reason, like someone is visiting. They want to feel safe at home – physically and virtually. They want to live in a home that is comfortable and productive, where they have time for personal life and hobbies. Assisted by tech, they work from home, order food for delivery, and binge watch their favourite streaming shows. Things that could make their life better are reminders for daily tasks, automated support for home cleaning and organizing, flexible space for different activities and any form of help to manage their work–life balance.

Three key themes

As we worked through these eight mindsets, three psycho-social headline themes emerged that need to be kept in mind by providers of tech, services and products for Future Home markets. The first is 'identity', as that impacts the meaning of home. The second is 'spatial revolution', focused on multipurpose needs in today's home and evolving to feeling at home anywhere. The third is 'tech tensions', which looks at how people adapt to and struggle with more new technologies.

Identity

Our sense of self is intertwined with the home. As the eight mindsets in our typology show, we all have distinct ideas about what home means and how it feels to us individually. From these various perspectives, we look differently at needs such as safety, comfort and being in control. The business opportunity is finding ways to adapt the design of the Future Home to these different notions of what home means for each mindset and how they may change over time with life events such as having children, changing jobs, semi-retirement, or becoming a grandparent.

The first thing the home needs to be is comfortable. Comfort could mean anything from access to pictures of friends and family to space that allows you to be yourself without judgment. For a Drone Parent it is a need to be private and secure, with all the essentials. For a Savvy Senior it is a place for reflection and recognition, with life achievements on display. For Ambience Leaders it is a unique and joyful place to rest and rejuvenate. For a Social Grandparent it is a warm, cosy place to gain respite from a busy day.

Then there is safety, itself commanding a wide spectrum of understanding across the eight mindsets. Feeling safe doesn't necessarily just come from a deadbolt on the front door or a high-tech security system. Sometimes it comes from being surrounded by one's favourite things in a pleasant environment. For a Hip-happening Parent the idea of safety is a physical alarm system and being surrounded by family. For a Drone Parent it is having a physical security system and being monitored by carbon monoxide and fire safety detectors. For a Savvy Senior and a Social Grandparent it is all about the location and neighbourhood.

Being in control is similarly different for different mindsets. For some, apps and devices act as empowering tools. For others, being in control means having a clean and organized space and the ability to maintain a simple daily ritual. For a Social Grandparent it is about the smartphone that keeps her or him connected to friends and family. For the Chaotic Creative it could be having a morning coffee ritual while checking favourite websites. For Ambience Leaders it might be the voice assistant that enables productivity.

Spatial revolution

The idea of traditional space use within a home is disappearing as more and more tech comes into homes. Open, multi-purpose rooms are becoming common, used for activities like eating, exercising, sleeping, working and more. With the 'always-on' approach to employment, and the popularity of working from home on certain days, the boundaries between home and office blur.

Homes therefore need to be fluid and flexible to respond to these changing needs. This tech-driven spatial revolution does not dictate physical demarcations anymore. The use of connected devices in the home means people can be in the same physical space but also inhabit other realms, for example via social media in cyberspace or through a volumetric digital twin.

After the Future Home is harmonized and the existing spaces become more multi-purpose, it will evolve in a second phase in which parts or rooms of the home become monetizable assets that can be rented to others for set periods of time.

The Future Home could then enter a third and final phase, 'at home anywhere', freeing users from the physical walls of home. This is the true realization of hyper-connected living. You will be able to bring your personal photos and preferences into an autonomous car on your way to work. You will be able to rent out your home in a shared economy while you are out of town on a work trip staying in a hotel but also projecting all the feeling of your home into the hotel room. The theme of identity becomes clearest in its importance here: using true human understanding to guide new disruptive technologies such as 5G, big data analytics and edge computing will mean you can bring the identity of your home and your own sense of identity, which depends on it, into any other given space.

Tech tensions

The rapid advances in tech potentially bring many benefits and much increased flexibility to home life. Nevertheless, we often choose to stick to inflexible daily habits and despite the massive advances in technology, people's routines are still often low-tech and traditional. They wake to an analogue bedside alarm, make coffee on the stove, commute using trains, buses or bicycles, come home, walk the dog, tend the garden, go for a run, watch TV and so on.

Too much tech, front and centre commanding attention, can cause discomfort and distress, with many confused by multiple devices in their homes. We believe that anyone creating products and services for the Future Home in 5G needs to understand and rationalize these tensions, while still using tech to enhance experiences around daily routines and rituals for users.

Technology and social media create an instant connection to the world outside the home. Messenger groups, tracking apps and video calls make this easy. But this can also have destructive effects on people by cutting them off from the community they live with at home or just around the corner. We need to step back and look at the tensions intelligent devices create in homes and users. Balancing this with different experiences at home will be hugely useful and good business for home tech providers. Together we can remove 'alone together'.

Another issue we need to think through is related to security and privacy, especially with regard, again, to the proliferation of multiple interconnected devices at home. There is a massive trust issue to manage for home tech providers in relation to end users.

The trends, personas and themes highlighted in this chapter form a foundation for thinking about the direction of new business models around the Future Home.

Takeaways

1 Megatrends such as the emergence of hyper-connected lifestyles, the tech savviness of younger generations, ageing in place and a 'do it for me' attitude will define variations of the Future Home market.

2 The specific mindsets of all sorts of Future Home user types can be pinpointed as a distinct mix between 'Showstoppers', 'Nestlers', 'Explorers' and 'Navigators'.

3 Businesses catering to the Future Home market should take socio-demographic types as the starting point for technological solutions – not the other way around.

3

From use cases to business cases

CHAPTER SUMMARY

....

We have just seen how diverse the sociology of domestic life in the Future Home will be. Different socio-demographic resident groups will sometimes need very different technology stacks backing up services specifically tailored to their needs. It is therefore worth looking at two more daily domestic life scenarios, one that is not only confined to a single person but involves a whole family (the Hip-happening Parent type) and one that entails ageing in place and advanced home care (Drone Parents and Social Grandparent). In both cases Future Home technology must be intelligent and responsive enough to identify different household members and their individual needs and preferences, but also to communicate meaningfully with service providers from outside the home and even with other Future Homes. Both use cases are still on the drawing boards of Accenture's 5G Future Home teams. But they stand a good chance of becoming real-life business cases very soon.

....

Life scenario 1: Home life for the Hip-happening Parents

It's late afternoon in a single-family home in a suburban neighbourhood. Paul and Susan live here with their three children: Winnie (2 years old), Eaton (6 years old) and Katherine (10 years old). With a full house, luckily the yard is being quietly clipped by an autonomous lawnmower. This frees young father Paul to spend precious moments with the family's two-year-old toddler, whom he is teaching to count. The numbers 1 to 5 seems to stick with the little girl without a problem, but 6 to 10 still present a challenge.

Intelligent assistance with childcare

Susan calls for her husband from the hallway entrance. Paul leaves Winnie with a smart toy panda. 'Carry on teaching numbers from 6 to 10, please', he tells it. The cute panda robot steps in as educator immediately, saying 'Hi Winnie' to the toddler. Then it plays her a video in which 10 coloured sticks are laid out one at a time, encouraging Winnie to touch sticks 6 to 10, while the numbers are sung to music.

Hassle-free plug-and-play technology

Earlier, six-year-old Eaton had thrown a ball at the ceiling, unfortunately breaking both the connected smoke detector and the connected camera. The digital assistant sensed the sound and realized the connected smoke detector and connected camera were not online. The digital assistant then analysed the last few seconds of the connected camera video to see a ball approaching the lens at high speed. The digital assistant then asked Susan if she would like to order both replacements. Susan agreed and both devices were drone-delivered within an hour of ordering. 'There's no need to read the label and check compatibility since all of these devices are connected to one harmonizing 5G wireless network.

I'm relieved that we changed the plan with our provider to a Future-Home-as-a-Service model', Susan says to Paul, who holds the stepladder as his wife climbs up to simply plug in the new devices.

The job takes 45 seconds. As per Susan's comments, the devices are easy, plug-and-play items, slotted in and ready to go. The family's Future Home recognizes both hardware devices instantly, connects them to the network and adds them to the monthly Future-Home-as-a-Service account. From the first moment of connection, both new replacement devices talk to all hardware and software components they need to in order to deliver a seamless user experience of service and quality to the family. All this is possible because the devices are fitted with smart algorithms and work on standard protocols agreed across the hardware industry. Paul and Susan are happy to pay for such advanced service levels when it means technology causes them no hassles. No need for a head-scratching solution architect to spend time pondering the compatibility of products, connecting device by device manually to Wi-Fi routers or to other hub devices via complex set-up procedures.

The home that knows each inhabitant personally

Meanwhile Katherine, the eldest, is in the common living space and the digital assistant has recognized her. It knows her homework has been completed because it helped her upload it to the school cloud folder, so, using its camera-equipped voice assistant, it asks her if she wants to play a game. 'Do you want to pick up from where you left off [on the smartphone during the autonomous bus ride home from elementary school]?' Katherine just nods and the game starts. Now that she's home, the walls display the game around the entire room, immersing Katherine, and there are no console boxes to plug into the TV, and no wires or inputs to figure out.

At the same time Paul is in the kitchen. He takes the milk from the fridge and pours himself a glass, feeling not an ounce of guilt about finishing the carton. He knows that the optical-sensor-fitted refrigerator, connected to the Future Home's visual data insight centre, has instantly added milk to the shopping list that will be delivered just before dinner time. Then, the Future Home security system makes an announcement: 'A stray cat with a clipped ear has entered the backyard'. In video displayed on the refrigerator door, the cat is about to use the newly planted flower-bed as a litter box. The Future Home chases the animal off by emitting a repellent sound. 'Stray cat has been shown the exit', the system tells Paul.

The home health check-up

In the meantime, Susan has her basic annual physical examination. She goes into a small, designated room in the Future Home and closes the door. Instantly her general care physician appears on the interactive walls. 'Hi, Susan, how are we today?' she says. The vitals are taken in real time and sent to the digital health register that the doctor sees: her weight is measured by the pressure on floor sensors, the pulse and blood pressure from her smart watch, the body temperature from room sensors. Paul and Susan have bought this basic service from their CSP who bundles all Future Home services for them. The 'Remote Physical – Basic' package is a service offered in partnership between the CSP and the family's health insurance, which grants policy rebates when customers' health test results are good. 'All clear. As we discussed, I'll order the vitamin D pills via a drone and see you in a year's time,' says the doctor.

Taking home with you wherever you go

Seeing health personnel at home allows more time for enjoying extra family life. Susan and Paul decide to take the kids to a new theme park. When Paul goes to get Winnie ready, he sees that the smart panda has moved on to the numbers 10 to 15 – and he knows it wouldn't have done this unless Winnie's results for learning 6 to 10 were perfect. 'Great, Winnie, soon you will be able to count up to my age', says Paul.

Meanwhile, Susan has finished reprimanding Eaton for throwing the ball in the house and has disengaged Katherine from her immersive game, and they all hop in the autonomous vehicle. The Future Home notices the family leaving and locks itself. 'I'll see you tonight. House and surroundings secured. And I'll keep an eye out for that stray cat looking for bathroom breaks,' the system tells the family as they roll down the driveway. Paul is impressed by their Future Home's conversational skills and even sense of humour.

In the back of the vehicle, Winnie is playing a location-based game in augmented reality (AR) overlaid on the car windows. It teaches her how to count the buildings, and spells out for her the things she is counting, like doors, windows and buildings. Katherine is meanwhile continuing a version of her streaming multi-player video game. Paul and Susan watch previews of the theme park rides with the shortest wait time while the autonomous vehicle safely navigates the family.

Fostering family togetherness

After 20 minutes, the Future Home notices that everyone has had enough solitary screen time, as per the settings Paul and Susan have previously agreed. It therefore sets things up for everyone to play together in the autonomous vehicle on all the windows. All five seats turn around creating a living-room setting in the autonomous vehicle and the family gets out a simple analogue board game.

Life scenario 2: Advanced healthcare at home

A Drone Parent couple, Mingteh and Sumei Wang, have three children with plenty of weekend activities such as piano lessons, soccer practice and drama classes. Given the Drone Parent's own busy working schedule, plus their kids' hefty after-school activities, there is literally no time left to make the eight-hour trip to check and see Mingteh's mother and the children's only living grandmother, YuPei, who lives 600 kilometres away in a rural area, more than once a year. This is especially worrying since the advanced-age grandmother lives on her own and just came home after a stroke that left her with only 70 per cent function on the left side of her body. After the stroke, she went from the hospital to an acute rehab centre to continue with physical therapy for the large muscle groups and occupational therapy for the small muscle groups before she was discharged home.

Freeing seniors to age at home

Since the Drone Parents find it difficult to consistently visit, and YuPei wants to 'age in place' – in her own home rather than in a nursing home – the Drone Parents need help from their Future Home. YuPei is a Social Grandparent type, mentally sturdy and in good spirits. 'I want to re-learn how to use the 30 per cent functionality I lost from head to toe. And I want to do that in my own home, living independently,' she had said after the stroke.

Mingteh and Sumei duly explained YuPei's situation to a representative from their CSP, Connect to Life (CTL). The representative replied that a local sub-acute rehab centre could offer the family an insurance-subsidized 'Ageing in Place 5G Future Home Solution'. This would be installed, billed and managed by the CSP, there would be a revenue share with the insurance provider and the local sub-acute rehab facility would daily monitor the data transmitted by the solution from a medical rehabilitation point of view.

The family and CTL arranged for the monthly recurring payments from the Drone Parent's account and privacy and security consent forms were signed by both the Drone Parents and the Social Grandparent. Then an appointment was made for the DIFM installation of the 'Ageing in Place 5G Future Home Solution' in the Social Grandparent's home. With this done, her previously rudimentary home became a Future Home in 5G.

Adapting an old home for new needs

The solution comprises a robotic assistant fitted with sensors, cameras with video analytics, microphones, a smart pill dispenser, exercise mirrors and connected TV integration. When YuPei wakes up each day, there is a robotic walking assistant that greets her in the comfort of her home and helps her to steady her body out of bed. The robotic assistant leverages computer vision and AI in near real time over a 5G network to react to and support the Social Grandparent.

Since she has only 70 per cent usage of her left leg, it still takes time getting used to it all. But Mingteh and Sumei can rest assured that there is very limited fall risk and if it should happen, the nearby rehab centre will instantly be alerted and send help.

'She is making outstanding progress,' the local doctor tells the family during a recent bi-weekly video call, 'She made a short trip to the local shop for the first time the other day.' The Drone Parents and, more importantly, the doctors, get a progress report relating daily distances walked, and measurements for stability and pace of movement. This data feeds right back into the Future Home system where the action of the robotic walking aid is recalibrated accordingly to provide less and less support as YuPei builds her strength back up.

Keeping in touch with a grandparent via technology

YuPei has dubbed her robotic assistant 'Butler'. At the start of the day, 'Butler' helps her get dressed, selecting outfits for her that have been cleaned, pressed and folded the night before. While she dresses, her Future Home projects a feed of the last 24 hours' social media posts onto the walls of the bathroom. Through gestures and voice, she can like or comment and generally keep up with her family, and keep them up to date with her. 'I told "Butler" today that I might be laying him off soon, as I might not need him anymore,' she says, dictating a social media post under a selfie of her and the robotic assistant, 'But I told him that he can stay around.'

Constant health monitoring and maintenance

After her monitored and assisted walk to the bathroom and the morning tooth brushing, a set of sensors in the sink analyses her discarded saliva for signs of overall health and any disease progression. This data is relayed to the local rehab centre for automated screening.

In the meantime, the kitchen prepares breakfast from tailored diet components delivered each morning. A camera with video analytics tracks how much of each meal YuPei consumes. The system also leverages 5G and edge computing technology to spot in near real time any chewing or swallowing issues on her left side, which could signal another medical issue such as a second stroke.

After breakfast, YuPei is reminded to take her high blood pressure medication and blood thinners, each from the smart pillbox that manages the amount, adherence or reduction of each medication, sending the information to the doctor, insurance company or pharmacy for a monthly discount incentive. When YuPei looks at the smart exercise mirror, the voice of a personal trainer takes her through a stroke recovery routine. The mirror shares results and data from the occupational therapy, physical therapy, and cognitive tests with a federated cloud that helps analyse progress and adjusts the training routines based on that progress. Once the exercises are over, the mirror turns into a screen for her personal family channel. YuPei sees a stream of pictures, messages, videos, and live streams from the Drone Parents' home, mobile devices and autonomous vehicles – including her grandchildren's phones.

Takeaways

1 Modern life is busy and therefore people are keen to automate mundane tasks, resolve current issues and predict future risks. To match these demands, home technology must be tailored to residents' real needs in order to be effective.

2 Convenience and hassle-free plug-and-play functionality creates optimal user experience.

3 Thoughtfully applied, tech can bond people at home rather than rendering them 'alone together'.

4 Future Home use cases can also relieve the pressure on society: ageing in place in the Future Home, for example.

4

Turning homes into 5G Future Homes

CHAPTER SUMMARY

....

The real-life examples in Chapters 1 and 3 have illustrated the huge benefits Future Home technology can have for the lives of many different groups of people. But for this potential to be realized, the shortcomings of previous attempts by businesses at pulling off the connected home must be overcome. Strong fragmentation of hardware and software standards, point-to-point architectures and heavy data siloing still present stubborn barriers. Soon though, 5G in combination with technologies such as eSIM, edge computing and advanced analytics will fix these problems, allowing the Future Home markets to prosper and grow dramatically. In this chapter, we explain what makes 5G not just a step up from previous cellular standards, but a generational leap with the power to transform the way we live and entire industries. While this requires going into more technical detail than elsewhere in the book, we think many readers will find it helpful in understanding 5G's unique capacity to deliver the Future Home.

....

The decade of evolving digital home technology is a history of repeated failures to create a well-rounded and therefore mass-adopted connected home experience. Information technology architectures and connectivity have been too patchy and makeshift, resulting in wild device ensembles in the home with narrowly pointed solutions focused on single problems – hardly the foundations for attractive mass adoption and user experiences to meet the consumer DIFM mega trend.

Yes, there are now connected thermostats that learn and help consumers save energy. And yes, video-enabled doorbells now provide safety, and connected home assistant speakers make getting information easier at home. And some home connectivity hub solutions have received good reviews, integrating several of the wireless technologies used in homes. But the overall reality of this device zoo is sobering, given the ways they could all come together so much more effectively to create a truly wonderful and life-enhancing experience within the Future Home.

The limited success so far of connected home tech

Looking at the players that will be key to Future Homes – communications service providers (CSPs), platform and app providers and hardware manufacturers – none have yet overcome all the critical hurdles to drive mass-market adoption.

The CSPs, as we said in the introduction, can be a lightning rod for much-needed change in the home. Many, however, have essentially launched their home offerings without first finding the right partners. Note that CSPs were entering the home market from a position of strength: the enormous advantages of their traditional role as providers of 'last-mile' connectivity into homes – the very final leg of the connectivity value chain connecting homes with broadband data. CSPs also have direct customer relationships and hence massive distribution power, and they still score extraordinarily highly in consumer trust rankings for reliability and security.[1] Nevertheless, the lack of partnerships means they have been unable to capitalize on this position. The companies with whom they would have needed to work, such as hardware manufacturers, were in their infancies and without them there was simply no way to provide an adequate suite of truly harmonized and connected solutions.

In contrast, when the platform and app providers were ready to make their moves into early home tech markets, they had success by entering with hardware. Initially this hardware focus was on adding connectivity to existing home equipment such as the doorbell or creating new devices such as the connected speaker unlocking a digital assistant. If we think of Google/Nest's thermostats or Amazon's Echo speakers, they are success stories in terms of solutions with a focus to solve comparably narrow problems in the home. But hardware was not the primary target. The platform providers leveraged this new hardware to help gather more data in the early home market to feed into their core business models of data monetization. By nature, these platforms depend upon plenty of user data to understand the right context and deliver recommendations.

Again, it is important to note that it was expensive for platform and app providers to enter a new market like home tech. They had to build or acquire hardware development capabilities to make this a success, committing huge investment budgets. Amazon built Lab126, and Google strategically acquired home tech specialist Nest for US $3.2 billion.[2] Yet, even after building a capability internally or via strategic acquisition, there is still a need for partnerships to enable various development processes for devices, such as hardware design and engineering, software development and integration, direct customer access, distribution channels, and networks. And most importantly, platform providers do not currently have access to data on other devices or in other ecosystems that they have not created partnerships with yet. Early on, platform providers focus on product development to capture market share; a by-product of this could be less initial focus on sharing information with others.

Finally, there are the pure hardware manufacturers who also struggled with the current connected home. Often the business model and industry maturity of traditional home devices such as TVs and large appliances brought on commoditization. They found themselves in very mature markets where price was becoming one of the few differentiating factors. With few choices as margins continued to erode, the hardware manufacturers started to target specific customer segments using existing hardware, but with increased personalization and added features such as connectivity, to unlock new use cases such as the connected video doorbell; or they created entirely new markets such as connected speakers. But the issue for them was still that the traditional hardware and device manufacturers did not own strong software development or ecosystem development capabilities.

Next to CSPs and hardware manufacturers, there are the platform creators and the app and content managers, both dependent on what data insights they have been able to gather in the early home tech market. Again, the rewards have been very limited. Why? Because device manufacturers pursued proprietary approaches with their point-to-point solutions, sharing hardly any data with other platforms.

Signify, formerly Philips Lighting, a manufacturer of luminaires, LEDs and lighting solutions, is a still rare positive example of a hardware maker that, as a matter of strategy, makes its data available for third-party usage. Signify was one of the few traditional hardware players able to build software and create a data platform. The company has created an open ecosystem giving away this data so that third-party applications can be developed that will play on Signify hardware. In principle, this hardware can connect and provide data to all other connected devices, very similarly to the multi-sided Android operating system that makes data available in all directions, providing interoperability between all other connected devices.[3]

There are other alternatives for hardware manufacturers. They could follow the example of Apple, where the hardware creator is the orchestrator and decides who can work with shared data. Or they might establish a platform mechanism using blockchain technology that allows the original data creators to give controllable permission for further use by individually selected third parties.

Regardless of the starting positions of CSPs, platform providers or hardware manufacturers, everyone in the connected ecosystem remained bound to the connectivity constraints of the pre-5G era. Wi-Fi has been the prevailing wireless connectivity standard in most homes. Similar unlicensed personal area network technology like Zigbee or Z-Wave have also popped up but require another hub in addition to a Wi-Fi gateway already demanding space in each home. Hardware makers have tried to make the best of this and used Wi-Fi and low-power personal area networks as their 'best effort' connectivity proposition. While Wi-Fi-based technologies are cheap, they are not reliable enough or secure enough to really offer watertight private and secure service experiences at home.

This kind of fragmented connectivity also inhibited data flow and data pervasiveness at times. Data pervasiveness is a crucial factor for orchestrating quality service offerings that anticipate consumer behaviour. To put it in concrete terms, a home setting must be so interconnected that it is able to draw its own conclusions from a wide range of its data-driven 'observations'. Why, for instance, should the vacuum cleaner not be allowed to start work at 8 am today? Because the Future Home connected a few pieces of data: the shower wasn't running at the usual time, the thermostat temperature was raised above the normal level and also sensed that somebody had moved around the bedroom several times at night, the connected speaker assistant had been consulted about muscle aches, the intelligent pill box knew ibuprofen had been taken and the Department of Health had reported a flu outbreak at a nearby elementary school where the inhabitant works. From all these secondary inputs, the primary conclusion is drawn that the home inhabitant is going to be ill in bed today, so the noise and disruption of vacuuming can wait a day or two. The inhabitant can then sleep peacefully without even worrying that the ordinary routine is going to disturb this much needed recovery and rest. But this advanced level of data sharing and correlation requires standardization, business model incentives and value chain benefits for all.

In addition to all the fragmentation among CSPs, hardware manufacturers and platform providers, there have also been the kind of teething problems one would expect with any new tech: smart doorbells mistaking a wind-blown bush for activity at the front door and constantly sending video clips of a moving bush while the user is in an important meeting. Or smart speakers waking up and reacting mistakenly to something on a television programme and blaring a response while an infant fell asleep.

Beyond that, there are four further obstacles that have prevented connected home technology and service providers from living up to consumer expectations and thus developing a reasonable and coherent Future Home tech market. In order to understand how they might be overcome – with the crucial assistance of 5G – it will be instructive to look at them in detail.

Excessive connected home device prices

The first obstacle is initial cost. There tends still to be a massive difference in price between non-connected and connected devices. Figure 4.1 gives some instructive examples.

Figure 4.1   Price comparisons between connected and non-connected devices[4]

Home Device	Non-connected	Connected	Approximate $ Diff	Percent Increase
Refrigerator	$ 2,000.00	$ 3,500.00	$ 1,500.00	75%
Door lock	$ 35.00	$ 150.00	$ 115.00	329%
Light bulb	$ 2.00	$ 10.00	$ 8.00	400%
Door bell	$ 16.00	$ 130.00	$ 114.00	713%
Vacuum	$ 50.00	$ 500.00	$ 450.00	900%
Electrical outlet	$ 1.00	$ 15.00	$ 14.00	1400%
Thermostat	$ 14.00	$ 250.00	$ 236.00	1686%

To sum up: on average, today's connected devices – from refrigerators to thermostats – can be between 150 and around 2,000 per cent more expensive depending on the type of hardware. These price differences have often been justified, as cutting-edge technology and components such as processors, sensors and AI software are built into the connected devices, with each component itself carrying a heavy price tag.

But the high price differentials are unlikely to last for successful connected devices. Once consumers decide a connected home device adds value, demand will increase and economies of scale will bring device prices down. For example, televisions are not listed in the table because it's now hard to actually buy a non-connected television. And if you do find one, the price difference is minimal compared to a connected TV.

However, the clear value propositions required to reach scale depend on an efficient orchestrator to help harmonize the home experience provided by all devices. This is what will allow them to become part of smarter homes, then more automated homes and finally the Future Home that will be predictive, think for its resident and allow the resident to feel at home anywhere.

Impractical set-up procedures

The second obstacle to the Future Home is impracticality. In today's home tech world, it is not at all easy to build a tailored stack for your home. Each device requires a different set-up, and plug and play is almost nowhere to be found.

On average, consumers invest 2.5 hours in set-up and customer support, and speak with three different people to resolve connected home set-up issues, according to iQor's Customer and Product Experience 360 Survey.[5] The connected home was meant to make our lives simple but setting one up turns out to be a DIY project that can be wildly complicated. Market researchers Parks Associates found that 28 per cent of smart home device owners rated the set-up process as either difficult or very difficult.[6] The same report found that when DIY consumers are asked how they would like to install future devices (regardless of the cost involved), 41 per cent indicate they would prefer some form of technical assistance.

In other words, people want DIFM over DIY, especially in the Future Home. According to a recent Accenture survey of more than 6,000 people across 13 countries, mentioned in Chapter 2, only 25 per cent of consumers of connected home products and services consider themselves Explorers, active lead adopters of new technology, products and services. Based on the same survey, 63 per cent are more trend-lagging Navigator types, who will only be persuaded to live in a Future Home when things are easy, proven by others and assembled for them.[7]

So today's connected home is stuck in the early pioneer phase of the technology adoption curve and struggling to move on to mass-market acceptance.

Fragmentation

The third hurdle standing in the way of a thriving Future Home market is tech fragmentation. Home connectivity has historically been built to solve very specific use cases. In waves of uncoordinated expansion, this brought a variety of technologies and standards into homes. Devices use different standards, spectrum frequency bands or data rates, travel different distances, require different power usage, and cost different amounts of money to integrate.

In today's connected homes, a handful of radio standards work side by side without connection: Wi-Fi standards next to ZigBee standards next to Z-Wave standards next to cellular standards and more. There are just too many different communication protocols and technology profiles in use that do not communicate and data-inform each other – something that is holding back mass adoption of seamless Future Home solutions.

This simply creates too much friction for a convincing value proposition to consumers. For user experiences to be excellent, home tech must be able to sense all, comprehend all, act and learn from everything that happens in the Future Home. That makes cutting-edge technologies such as artificial intelligence (AI) indispensable. For the purposes of this book, when we discuss AI, we mean a collection of technologies that can enable a machine or system to sense, comprehend and act. These AI technologies include, but are not limited to basic pattern matching, machine learning, computer vision, natural language processing and applied analytics. But these advanced technologies require pervasive data flows and access to a massive amount of unstructured and structured data.

One can see, then, the need for universal connectivity. This is now a reality in the form of the 5G standards. When all devices and services can easily talk to each other and share data, we are well on our way to making the connected home the Future Home.

The weaknesses of Wi-Fi

The fourth hurdle for thriving Future Home markets is today's wide use of the Wi-Fi wireless standard in homes. This free-of-charge wireless access technology typically rides on top of a paid-for home broadband connection, a so-called 'last-mile' wiring into homes, typically comprised of coaxial cable, fibre-optic or copper-based asymmetric digital subscriber lines (ADSL), all eventually connected to a core network.

Wi-Fi architectures involve a few points of failure, making the technology unreliable and sometimes less secure compared to 5G. The free availability of the unlicensed spectrum can, for instance, turn into a disadvantage in densely populated areas – such as cities or even apartment blocks, where too many participants can start fighting for Wi-Fi spectrum, taking up available channels, slowing down the overall system and also leading to interference of the different user devices. Even the newest Wi-Fi 6 and Wi-Fi HaLow standards are prone to congestion and interference problems. For instance, Wi-Fi HaLow may still experience interference since it shares a bandwidth with several other home devices such as cordless phones, lighting controls or augmented reality equipment.

There are further drawbacks with Wi-Fi in general. For instance, when the power cuts off, a user cannot be sure that all Wi-Fi devices will reconnect automatically once the power comes back on. This is because today's connected devices are all made by different manufacturers and thus have different design and antenna placements or component qualities. That said, even with 5G, technology devices are not 100 per cent guaranteed to come back to service autonomously without any further resetting action after power cuts.

Another disadvantage of Wi-Fi is simply the short range. As just noted, Wi-Fi uses unlicensed and shared spectrum bands, typically in the 2.4 GHz to 5 GHz range. What that means in practical terms is that Wi-Fi signals travel only short distances, resulting in Wi-Fi 'dead zones' or very low signal areas in some parts of the home. On top of this, Wi-Fi broadband modem routers are rarely updated with the latest hardware or software, leading to quickly ageing hardware and all the accompanying data security threats.

Data travels on Wi-Fi networks only between device and router. It is then fed into a fixed-line network that constricts and impacts the speed of the service, particularly where last-mile connectivity is a legacy telephone line (copper bottleneck). A gardener digging in the front yard could accidentally sever your broadband line. Some devices would still indicate a full Wi-Fi connection, but your actual connectivity would not work.

Finally, there is also Wi-Fi's relatively long response time. For example, each internet service provider must build, lease or partner with a set of long-haul fibre network providers or interconnect providers to reach the internet. Most Wi-Fi home solutions use the touch of a smartphone icon or your voice via a smart speaker as controller. This signal still has to pass many handover points to reach a connected home device – which is why conventional Wi-Fi connections have such long latency. Latency refers to the lag between stimulation and response – literally, between the time you press a button and the time it takes for that to activate something. You might have wondered why it takes a few seconds or more after you ask your connected speaker voice assistant to turn on

Figure 4.2   **Potential connection failure points in a typical Wi-Fi/Zigbee/Z-Wave connected home**

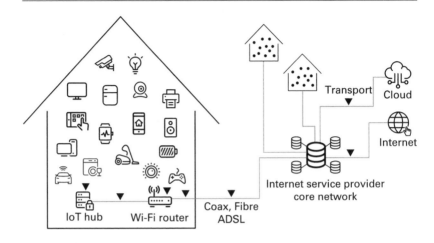

Internet service provider
core network

Transport

Cloud

Internet

IoT hub   Wi-Fi router   Coax, Fibre
ADSL

▼ Potential points of failure, including unlicensed and shared spectrum subject to interference and congestion

your room lights for the action to be carried out. It's simply because the request has to jump through many hoops on its way from command to action. Figure 4.2 shows that there are several points of potential failure along a typical Wi-Fi home connection.

And when you compare Wi-Fi to licensed cellular technologies such as the currently prevailing 4G LTE cellular phone standard (see Figure 4.3), it becomes evident how cellular has the advantage in network reliability, security, mobility and roaming. Coverage range alone makes the case for cellular connectivity a consideration: 50 metres (approximately) for Wi-Fi compared with 16,000 metres for cellular.

Still, Wi-Fi technology has a very important point working in its favour – lower cost. As a freely available spectrum, from the perspective of the user, it can probably be marketed much more easily than 5G, which is sold to end users like a running mobile phone contract on flat rates, or volume tariffs with payable monthly instalments, volume-based plans or by a connection fee to share data.

Figure 4.3   Comparing Wi-Fi with 4G LTE[8]

	2.4 GHz Wi-Fi	5 GHz Wi-Fi	4G LTE
Technology standard	802.11b/g/n	802.11b/g/n/ac/ax	3GPP Releases 8–15
Spectrum bands	2.4–2.5 GHz	5 GHz	Sub 6 Ghz
Max. data rate (download)	450–600 Mbps	up to 1300 Mbps	~1000 Mbps
Coverage range	~40 metres (indoors)	~15–20 metres	3000–16000 metres
Reliability	Medium	Medium	High (99.999% reliable)
Security	Medium	Medium	High (encrypted)
Mobility	Low (metres)	Low (metres)	High (kilometres)

How 5G can turn the connected home into the Future Home

Roughly every 10 years there is a new generational leap in cellular technology. 5G, as the name suggests, is the fifth generation of cellular technology and with the current 3GPP release 15 standard, 5G promises three important improvements over its predecessor, 4G:

- 10 Gbps peak data rates for enhanced mobile broadband (eMBB);

- 1 million connections per square km for massive Internet of Things (mIoT);

- 1 ms latency for ultra-reliable low-latency communications (URLLC).[9]

These theoretical 5G performance increases provide a massive opportunity for all sorts of industries but especially the ones cooperating in a Future Home ecosystem.

Figure 4.4 shows what predecessor cellular standards were able to deliver and that wireless connectivity was for a long time dedicated to voice and text traffic. From around 2019 the start of the mobile internet made much higher data capacity and speed necessary, both delivered now by 5G.

Figure 4.4   The increasing performance of each cellular generation[10]

1G	2G	3G	4G	5G
~1980	~1990	~2000	~2010	~2020
Mobile voice	Voice, text	Voice, text, data	Mobile internet	Greater speed, responsiveness and ability to connect more devices
<2 Kbps Analog Cellular	<64 Kbps GSM, TDMA, CDMA	<42 Mbps UMTS, HSPA, EVDO	<1 Gbps LTE, LTE Advanced	>10 Gbps 5G new radio, standalone core

New spectrum bands create high 5G speeds

New available spectrum bands and the amount available are what makes 5G wireless technology so powerful. In previous generations of cellular technology, there was no access to high-band spectrum between 24 GHz and 300 GHz. The availability and amount of this new spectrum, also called Millimetre Wave (mmWave), is a foundation of how 5G can deliver an exponential speed advantage over 4G.

However, while the amount of high-band spectrum is going to help increase bandwidth, speed and capacity, it sacrifices transmission distance. So successful 5G experiences will require a diverse mix of spectrum frequency bands: high-band, mid-band and low-band – all three defined by individual wavelengths.

Where waves belonging to the high-band spectrum are short and can reach very high speed combined with a high capacity, they can only travel short distances measured in metres. It is exactly the opposite with low-band waves that can travel far distances measured in kilometres. But there are not large amounts of spectrum for speed in low-band spectrum. As you can guess, the mid-band frequency offers a good mix between both capacity and coverage.

Accordingly, each of the three frequency bands suits a different use case and application purpose, which makes the 5G technology versatile. While high-band is good at covering urban areas with high data throughput capacity and short distances between a sending and receiving device, the mid-band spectrum – used so far in 2G, 3G and 4G predecessor standards – is best for applications in moving traffic, for example autonomous cars, and for sports stadiums and venues. The fact that low-band is best at penetrating walls and offers vast coverage would make it well suited for homes but also narrow valleys. Figure 4.5 shows the respective strengths of each spectrum band.

Figure 4.5   **Importance of diverse spectrum usage in 5G**

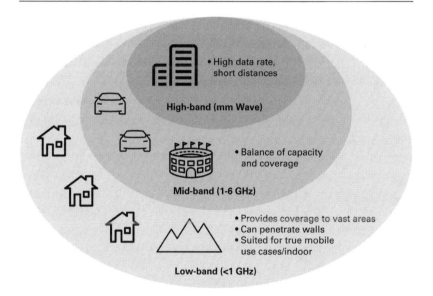

In the Future Home, many more things will be connected and some may not even require the same bandwidth that Wi-Fi provides so there will be a need for the transmission of data from low-power devices and sensors in the Future Home. The 3rd Generation Partnership Project (3GPP) is a standards body working on 5G standards. It has indicated that Narrow Band Internet of Things (NB-IoT), another designated spectrum, will also be part of the 5G standard to support low-power wide-area (LPWA) use cases. NB-IoT focuses on indoor coverage at a low cost using low power that can extend battery usage. NB-IoT is a technology that can transmit small data packets over long distances.

5G is more responsive and reliable

One of the most economically attractive things about 5G technology is the low latency driving high responsiveness of any applications in the Future Home. For perspective: a loaded 4G LTE network has an estimated latency of around 80 milliseconds. But to stream, for example, virtual reality or augmented reality to a head-mounted display requires lower latency: somewhere between 20 to 50 milliseconds to eliminate motion sickness. That's no problem with 5G; it can deliver a theoretical low latency of less than 1 millisecond. Figure 4.6 shows just what an advance this is, comparing 5G to other low-latency tech and natural phenomena, indicating the huge difference it will make to cutting-edge digital applications.

Figure 4.6 How 5G compares for latency

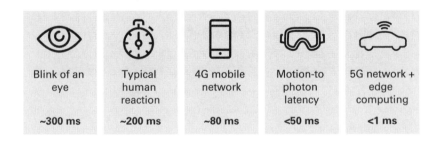

Blink of an eye	Typical human reaction	4G mobile network	Motion-to photon latency	5G network + edge computing
~300 ms	~200 ms	~80 ms	<50 ms	<1 ms

5G can, among other things, consolidate the speed of Wi-Fi with the low power consumption of ZigBee and Z-Wave standards into one wireless technology standard. This simplification to one connectivity standard can allow all devices on 5G to take advantage of 5G cellular's reliability compared to devices still on Wi-Fi, Zigbee or Z-Wave. Cellular technology is architected to be available up to 99.999 per cent of the time, meaning 5G cellular will on average be down only around 5.26 minutes per year. This level of reliability is especially important for critical communication areas such as remote surgery and autonomous driving, but also for the operation of medical monitoring devices at home.

5G can connect 10 times more devices than 4G

5G technology also has the potential to offer the foundational platform that is so urgently needed to transform the connected home into the Future Home by solving fragmentation. It can unify usage data in one place for the ecosystem to sense, comprehend, act on and learn from, so that the Future Home can deliver truly experience-rich services.

To give a flavour of what new business opportunities 5G offers, there will be 77 million US citizens aged 65 years and older by 2034, compared to around 76.5 million under the age of 18.[11] It will be the first time in US history that advanced-age adults outnumber minors. As we mentioned, ageing in place will be a very important feature of daily life over the coming decades, as more individuals attempt to maintain independence in advanced age.

It's hard to provide daily peace of mind to family members of loved ones who live far away. Continuous remote monitoring as we described in Chapter 3, of someone ageing in place, may require up to 100 connected devices to ensure a reliable, safe and predictive experience, or maybe even more. Let's break this down.

Up to 10 devices are needed to create enough safety and security for such a home – from high-resolution security cameras to smoke and CO_2 detectors to connected doorbells. Another dozen devices and sensors are needed to monitor nutrition and body weight – involving a connected refrigerator and connected pantry sensors and cameras that can help reorder food, as well as a connected scale.

It is further estimated that up to around 20 sensors and devices are needed to monitor an advanced-age person's health. Connected pill boxes, movement-tracking cameras, toilets and showers, connected blood pressure cuffs, oxygen monitors and thermometers fall into this category.

Up to around 50 further technology items are required to steer general daily life and ambient factors, ranging from connected thermostats to intelligent lighting plugs to connected speakers to air quality, moisture and motion sensors in all rooms, to entertainment features such as connected TV and other mobile devices such as laptops and tablets.

There are clear limitations on what Wi-Fi and 4G LTE technology can do to run such a complex set-up smoothly. Though in theory one Wi-Fi router could, in a standard version, connect that many devices at a time, the close proximity of each device would cause interference and performance issues because of all the devices having to go through just a few channels.

Even a 4G LTE wireless standard would have issues with densely connected devices at certain device and sensor saturations. Taking into account today's average US home size, one could fit around 4,360 homes per square kilometre. If these ageing-in-place homes each carry only around 50 connected devices or sensors, there could be a density of around 218,000 connected items per square kilometre. This would be twice as many devices as current 4G LTE networks can handle.

In contrast, 5G has no problem here. It can connect 1 million devices per square kilometre, which is more than enough to handle the device and sensor density in new ageing-in-place homes.[12]

5G's congenial enablers

While 5G will play a big role in removing the technology and data fragmentation of today's connected homes, harmonizing the various data-transmissions into one secure and reliable connection, it will need complementary technologies. The most important of these are eSIM, edge computing, and advanced analytics.

eSIM solves the size problem

In order for 5G to unlock ubiquitous connectivity, each connected home device needs the capability of a subscriber identification module (SIM) card, as is currently used in any smartphone to identify and connect the device to the network. A conventional SIM card stores the number and associated key to identify and authenticate subscribers. But smaller connected devices in the Future Home will have issues accommodating even the smallest SIM currently available.[13]

The solution is a so-called 'embedded SIM' or eSIM, which is soldered into the device and does not require a SIM card slot. eSIMs were developed by the industry body Global System for Mobile Communications Association (GSMA)[14] and are programmable, allowing people to store multiple user profiles on one single device or for a remote device to be set up with connectivity.

Edge computing removes network mileage

Recently computing power has largely moved to the cloud – providing remote and centralized computing capacity accessible through wired or wireless connections.

The centralized cloud concept is able to do great things, such as massive data processing as well as big data storage and analytics. But it also has limitations when it comes to the Future Home, with high latency and costs for transporting and relaying large amounts of data.

Enter edge computing. This is, in a nutshell, the renaissance of decentralized processing power. It is built on the creation of small, more local data centres that at the same time use some of the best aspects of the centralized cloud approach, such as processing power and storage. Essentially, it's part of the power and storage capacity with lower latency. This more local cloud enables faster response times and lower latency.

Remember the example of requesting a connected speaker to turn on the lights from the beginning of this chapter? The slow and unpredictable response is because the request travels from the speaker over Wi-Fi to the router, then through the broadband connection to the core network and finally all the way to a distant data centre. This data centre will then process the request to turn on lights and send the instructions all the way back again through the same complicated path to turn on each light. By contrast, 5G plus edge computing will simply do everything at a local and closer edge computing centre, making it much faster – a set-up that would admittedly also work with Wi-Fi in combination with edge computing.

Advanced data analytics for cleverer devices

The ability to transmit large amounts of data is all very well, but to really make use of it to determine the activities of your devices, you also need advanced data analytics.

Today's connected home solutions can already organize large amounts of data to match usage patterns. But these pattern-matching routines can actually frustrate you as used in today's connected homes. For instance, your living room thermostat may have established via pattern matching that you typically leave for work each morning at 8.30 am in the winter. It then turns the heat down to save money. But what about when you stay at home sick and don't want to have to get up to turn the temperature back up? Pattern matching will fail you.

This is where you need more data fed through advanced analytics tools to identify specific contexts and recommend the appropriate action. Simply put, the system must detect the times when you break your routine and stay at home.

Advanced data analytics can do exactly that as it offers a set of data-driven techniques that support fact-based and contextual decisions. Only 5G's low latency and high data capacity combined with advanced analytics can give your thermostat (and other devices) the necessary contextual response.

First steps: Mastering four challenges

To close this chapter, let's recap the four key challenges slowing down the Future Home and the 5G-enabled Future Home markets that so many industry participants would benefit from.

Challenge 1: Getting ecosystems right to lower the cost of Future Home devices

Businesses can and must work together to create the right Future Home ecosystem. This should ideally involve standardization of connectivity protocols and data exchange procedures for home tech devices, thereby ramping up purchase volumes of Future Home devices significantly. Bringing more partners together to buy in clusters, providing more accurate Future Home forecasts, and creating voluminous buying commitments will help hardware manufacturers to accelerate volume-driven price reductions.

Challenge 2: Leveraging 5G to solve set-up issues

Businesses need to better understand the new customers who will be the architects of the Future Home. Are they value-oriented and keen to spend time in order to save money or are they are convenience-oriented, willing to spend money to save time?

The answer is the latter. The Future Home architects will primarily be Millennials and Gen Z. They prefer DIFM over DIY and are willing to pay to make life easier.

So the big opportunity for businesses is to simplify the set-up process for home devices. They should use 5G to create a Future Home where you just turn on a device and it registers and works in a plug-and-play style, similar to when you power up your smartphone and it automatically connects to your cellular network. This is a big part of the convenience for which consumers will be willing to pay more.

But it will be critical, nevertheless, not to overprice services in the Future Home or select the wrong business model. Consumers do not want to pay another monthly subscription fee for each device added to the Future Home. Although CSPs have spent billions to acquire 5G spectrum licenses, it's understandable that they'd want to recoup this massive investment as soon as possible. They should, however, keep in mind that, as with connected devices, too high initial prices for home services can depress consumer enthusiasm, despite excellent user experience levels.

Challenge 3: Using 5G to solve the fragmented connectivity issues of today's homes

5G has the power to harmonize the fragmented wireless technologies in today's connected home and resolve the limitations of each wireless technology in use. It can consolidate the complex tangle of different radio standards such as mesh wireless protocols like Zigbee and Z-Wave, Wi-Fi (requires a lot of power) or Bluetooth (limited in number of devices connected) into one seamless and reliant connectivity solution. 5G also requires no physical modems, gateways or router boxes in the room.

Challenge 4: Uniting information pools and granting access for the greater good

Industries involved in Future Home development must co-create a common vision, business models and partnerships for collective data use focused on the user mindset and context. 5G connectivity can help unite all home devices, and even filter in data from pools and sources outside the home for more context. This data and information must be poured into a unified 'source of truth'. From this joint data lake, trusted partners can then help themselves to provide more relevant and personalized services to home users. This united information pool will be especially critical in realizing the Future Home's evolution – where you feel at home anywhere.

Takeaways

1 Today's connected homes harbour a plethora of incoherent device, protocol and radio standards that can be consolidated in one go by 5G.

2 5G and its segmented spectrum is ideally suited to create and enable new applications in the Future Home as it can fluidly balance speed, low latency and number of devices connected.

3 But 5G needs complementary technologies such as eSIM, edge computing and AI to reach its full experience potential.

5

Privacy and security: Two separate challenges of the 5G Future Home

CHAPTER SUMMARY

....

Initial worries over data privacy and data security are likely to hold back consumer trust around the Future Home. Today's connected homes are literally listening to us, but in a big leap forward the Future Home will also need to understand us in order to be able to think and act for us. The Future Home will therefore need to handle, process, store and secure enormous amounts of personal data. Meanwhile, 5G's ability to harmonize connectivity fragmentation, eliminate complex set-up issues, and remove data-sharing silos, will make the number of Future Home devices explode. A critical question is whether we have adequate privacy, security and regulation standards in place to handle the proliferation of these IoT devices. And are there AI technologies available that are 'ethical' enough to act with due responsibility on the behalf of Future Home users? We think that, across all use cases, the user's data sovereignty must be a priority for any Future Home value chain provider. And we think communications service providers (CSPs), as trusted brands and principal orchestrators of the Future Home, are best positioned to handle the protracted aspects of privacy and security.

....

As we have seen in the earlier chapters, user demands around the Future Home are changing dramatically, and the eight new user mindsets evolving, combined with the wider socio-demographic trends we described in Chapter 2, are providing input for the development of new business models for the Future Home. The 5G wireless standard – the central enabler of Future Home technology along with a few complementary technologies, as we described in the previous chapter – will bring about an explosion of connected devices and new business opportunities. It is estimated that the Internet of Things (IoT) will add an overall $14 trillion in economic value to the global economy by 2030, with a substantial share resulting from the new Future Home market.[1] Around the globe, tens of millions of homes will add more to the cache of connected devices they already have – a broad spectrum of always-on microphones, sensors, video cameras and data collecting and sharing mechanisms.

Furthermore, when Future Home users ground their home lives on ecosystems set up and run by providers in a DIFM fashion so that the Future Home can truly save them time and predict the next best action for each individual inhabitant, it will require the handling and processing of vast amounts of often very sensitive data. We have already mentioned several times how important trust will be in the relationship between Future Home users and their service providers. Any data privacy or data security breach would make this trust evaporate quickly and destroy a vast array of business opportunities. The proliferation of devices and the enormous amounts of data they share will, of course, dramatically increase the surface area for privacy breaches, irresponsible AI, and cybersecurity attacks. The bar for data security, privacy and ethical governance must therefore be set extremely high. To be able to offer a credible capability here will be a cornerstone of the Future Home's viability.

In meeting this challenge, it's important to understand that data privacy, data security and 'ethical AI', though closely related, are fundamentally different things.

- *Data privacy* refers to the right to control your own personal information and identity, including how your personal data is managed and used by parties beyond your own control.

- *Data security* refers to how your personal information is protected against unauthorized access.

- *Ethical and responsible AI* requires that devices within Future Home set-ups think and act along certain set moral boundaries.

These three topics are interlinked and we will discuss them as such. With regard to the last of these, it is indispensable that users are only exposed to unbiased and fair decision making, without the influence, for example, of societal bias or interested parties. All machine thinking and acting must also be both understandable and explainable, with solid reasoning behind its recommendations and actions. It must not take the non-repetitive or high-value decisions away from humans, but enhance the human capacity to decide and act, giving the user back control whenever required.

The paradox of the Future Home: Protecting data that must also be shared

Being delighted by the Future Home as a user means enjoying services hyper-personalized to your needs and based on situational context. But for this convenience, you will need to give up personal data. This effectively seems to mean trading your privacy for convenience and monetary savings. An oft-discussed idea in the digital world is that you 'pay' for such convenience with your usage data, an asset worth money to developers, advertisers and all other data-driven businesses in the value chain.

In a survey of 26,000 consumers in 26 countries, Accenture found that 73 per cent believe privacy issues are a barrier to the Future Home.[2] So how will service providers, or any other Future Home ecosystem partners for that matter, strike the right balance between collecting and processing data that is relevant to improving and personalizing the customer experience against all the concerns on a Future Home user's mind? And, secondly, how will they balance competitive pressures against responsible and ethical artificial intelligence/machine learning (AI/ML) architecture to keep the interests of the user at the heart of the matter? The latter question is the more difficult, as investments in and knowledge of AI technologies are concentrated within a few companies and in just a few countries initially competing fiercely against each other.

The need for privacy and responsibility will eventually be crucial even for data-liberal Millennials. Millennials and Gen Z will experience life events just as Gen X and Baby Boomers did before them. They will have children, rent or own homes and, in general, increase life responsibilities – and become more data-conservative in the process. Through each of these life stages, their trade-offs between offering data for convenience, experience or cost savings will change, something the ecosystem must bear in mind while building the Future Home in 5G. Data privacy and ethical behaviour will always be a moving target for digital service providers to the Future Home. It will require continuous analysis and care on their part for consumer trust to remain intact. And there is already some catching up to do, because for today's connected home users, the way their data is used is often not at all clear.

Meanwhile, data security is a prerequisite for the Future Home market to take off at all. Such a market simply could not work on the basis of security standards short of what users expect from their home today, where what is inside stays inside, and no outside party is allowed access to any asset – physical or data – without the user's consent. Let's look at this in more detail.

Data sharing in today's connected homes

Already in the connected homes of today, connected speaker digital assistants listen to what you, your family and friends say all through the day. They react to 'trigger' words or phrases that have previously been overheard, processed and stored.

It's no secret that you can, for example, go to your digital assistant's mobile application and listen to recordings of previous requests. You may think this is no big deal, reasoning that surely your requests are only for harmless things such as weather reports or playing music. But more and more personal data is amassed by these listening digital devices, some by accident, and it may be kept indefinitely. There may be items that are more security-sensitive than you notice. After all, you provided your home address during the digital assistant set-up process in order to allow it to estimate the length of your commute to work. Oops, there's another address you added and may have forgotten about: your work address. You also trained your digital assistant with your name and voice so it could distinguish your spoken requests from those of other family members or roommates in the same house – and for some reason, at the same time you also told it your birthday. You may even have provided financial or private medical information to enable some specific service. And while you may think it's funny if your voice assistant starts flirting with you – as many did in the early days of these applications – it won't be acceptable if this becomes a manipulative trait or biased behaviour on the part of the underlying AI/ML over time. In other words, it's not just an issue what the AI learns – though this is a big issue – it's also how it learns, what kind of behaviour it develops.

Multiply those connected speakers and digital assistants throughout the rooms of a home to increase convenience, productivity and time savings, and you increase the home's ability to listen to you even when you're not directly addressing the assistant and deliberately feeding it data. Again, many of those connected speakers and digital assistants will keep all the data they collect indefinitely and will constantly adapt their recommendations and actions to the user behaviour. They can very quickly become smarter about you than one of your friends or a significant human other.

This is because voice data is used to train natural language processing (NLP) systems and AI components to improve experience and, of course, heighten personalization. How long data is kept is one thing; who is allowed to use it is another. For instance, judicial authorities have forced digital platform and data service providers to hand over recordings made by connected speakers and digital assistants that might contain information on potential crimes. Amazon was compelled by the New Hampshire Superior Court to turn over recordings of its smart Echo speaker.[3] There is no easy way to reject such orders outside of the courts. Even where service providers try to prevent identification of user data via end-to-end encryption, governments and judicial authorities are increasingly becoming heavily involved in the data value chain, privacy and security, as they try to enforce access to this data.

Further examples of forced disclosure are easy to find. Between January and June 2017 alone, Facebook received 32,716 requests for disclosure of information from US law enforcement authorities. Google, in parallel, received 16,823 and Twitter 2,111 requests. Each company produced at least some information for about 80 per cent of the requests.[4] These requests are being made globally. In the first half of 2017, Amazon confirmed it had 75 requests from outside the United States based on a mutual legal assistance arrangement.[5]

Connected speakers and digital assistants are hardly the only connected home devices that are accumulating and storing your personal data. Connected thermostats track your movements when you get up at night so they can react accordingly. Connected lights in your bedroom can track when you sleep or wake, according to when each light is turned on or off. And connected vacuum cleaners use cameras and sensors to map your home's floor plan, while connected door locks produce detailed information on whether you are at home or not. While many companies providing such devices and services have privacy policies restricting how long personal data is kept, users wishing to speed up the process must either manually delete their personal data or ask for storage to be stopped.

The aim is a better user experience through personalization, but the knock-on effect is still that the data that fuels personalization gets stored. And as is probably clear to most people now, in the wrong hands, this vast amount of data literally hands over the keys to your home's front door, provides the ability to turn off or avoid security systems, and gives instructions on what part of your home can be attacked.

This is why both the ecosystem and users need to have a clear position on data privacy, security and storage. Users must be given control of their data and provided with clarity on their rights to it. They should in no uncertain terms be informed who uses it, how it will be used in service design, how long it will be stored, and ultimately how it will be secured against illicit misuse. They can then grant permission to pass it on.

We cannot keep burying these important points in legal small print that no one ever reads. Rather, the Future Home industry must provide transparent optional settings for users to choose from and support them with clearly intelligible legal terms. As well as providing privacy options, the Future Home must clearly explain how they will keep data secure. Users must not feel exploited and the use of their personal data must always be controlled by ecosystem partners directly on their behalf.

Fundamental business models may also need to be addressed in the Future Home with regards to user data. Today, a common business model to grow user scale on the internet is to offer a 'free' service that you do not directly pay for; instead your usage data is captured on a platform which then monetizes it through, perhaps, advertising. But there are other business models to consider in the Future Home. Paying directly for a service can reduce the incentive to sell data; even an equitable value exchange between ecosystem partners working to make our lives better in the Future Home could eliminate the need to sell data. It's important to note that business models can be multi-dimensional and change over time. But in order for the Future Home to fundamentally improve our lives and to move with us, the right business models, ones that promote the security of data, the sharing of data in the Future Home ecosystem, and the ethical use of that data, are critical.

CSPs are here in a great position to differentiate themselves for users. As orchestrators and gatekeepers to the end customer, unlike the providers of scale-driven, ad-supported business models, CSPs are less reliant on data monetization itself. The same goes for those providing connectivity devices for the home, such as routers, set-top boxes or smartphones. These can also offer services that manage identity, and encrypt data and information on the device, so that the data transmitted can only be associated to the user if he or she allows it.

Three touchpoints for CSPs to deal with data safety successfully

Huge advances in security technology and data protection have been made, but, despite these, security breaches have risen in recent years by more than 27 per cent. Ransomware attacks alone, where hackers hold data pending monetary payments, have doubled in frequency, from 13 per cent to 27 per cent.[6] No wonder some 65 per cent of Millennials are concerned that the data collected by connected devices is not handled properly and fear they could fall victim to security incidents or data breaches, or that their personal information could be sold to third parties.[7]

These statistics show that at today's technology levels an actor wanting to gain access via hacks or illicitly sold-on data to your home might succeed if the Future Home is not designed correctly. Elaborating on the previous example, the threats created are huge, as such a data intruder could get a detailed layout map of your home, hack your connected front door lock or garage opener, turn off your home's security alarm altogether, and disable any exterior security cameras. While the chance of this to happening to you might seem remote, there are real-world examples of extraordinary security vulnerabilities. Take the case of an attack suffered by a North American casino, which could easily be replicated in a home environment: the casino had an internet-connected fish tank that fed the fish automatically and monitored their environment. Hackers managed to break into the fish tank monitor and use this as an entry point into the company's systems, with the data then sent to hackers in Finland.[8]

These security breaches are good examples of the point made in Chapter 1: technological fragmentation, still widespread in today's connected homes, is prone to privacy and security breaches. The two cases underscore the need for a few large-scale Future Home orchestrators operating trusted data security standards with an end-to-end user view. But, crucially, recent data also shows a growing gap between the risks that organizations are assuming and their cybersecurity postures.[9] Put simply, the complexity of the offerings is outrunning the ability to manage their security. The closer we get to autonomously acting home services, the more service providers seem to feel ill-equipped to provide the necessary security standards. As Figure 5.1 shows, for all the relevant technologies, the protections currently fall short of protecting against the levels of risk.

Consumers therefore rightly continue to raise concerns about their privacy and security and the potential dangers of being connected. Connected device technology in the home and beyond has been ranked as a top factor in raising cybersecurity risks as such technologies become more and more widely adopted. In this light, data security can be

Figure 5.1   Gap between increased risk and cybersecurity protection[10]

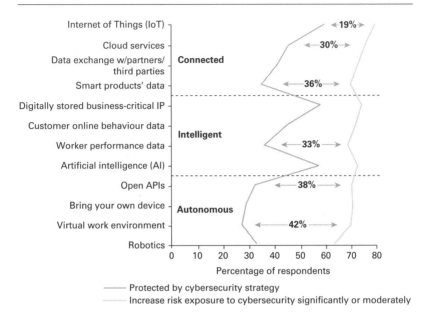

seen as a technology consideration with a truly human focus. This points to three clear touchpoints via which service providers as a sector can transform the security of the Future Home – unlocking benefits for both consumers and the broader ecosystem.

Cross-industry security certification for connected devices

When an individual makes an online purchase, creates an online account or engages with a service through their connected device, there is more than just an exchange of data, goods or services taking place. Another crucial exchange happens – of the ultimate currency in cyberspace: trust. At each of these interaction points, companies have an opportunity to validate and reward trust – strengthening their bond with the consumer and allowing product and service adoption to flourish – or violate and destroy it.

As should be clear by now, new intelligent connected devices in the Future Home will capture entirely new categories of data previously inconceivable. After all, more devices means more interconnections, which means more sharing of a broader range of data and insights. This increase in information and its flow will force service providers to massively increased levels of accountability for protecting the security and privacy of customer information. So in the current connected home and the Future Home in the 5G ecosystem, individual companies must not only consider the security of their own devices and services but also the risk of data breaches in companies with whom they are linked or partnered. Crucially, the ecosystem will not be able to reap its full benefits if consumers don't trust the entire value chain in which they operate.[11]

Unfortunately, not all organizations are equally prepared to deal with data security breaches. True, in a recent cross-industry report, Accenture found that the number of responding companies able to identify between 76 per cent and 100 per cent of breach attempts had more than doubled from the previous year to 23 per cent. Unfortunately, 24 per cent of organizations fell into the lowest category, only able to detect less than half of breach attempts.[12] This does not bode well for the Future Home in the 5G era. Given that the connected home proposition is only as strong as its weakest link, inconsistency in security posture will place massive limitations on overarching security and, as a consequence, hold back the emerging market around the Future Home.

A solution to the problem could be a certification framework for digital products, processes and services. It could be designed along the lines of Wi-Fi Certified, an internationally recognized certification of products indicating they meet industry-agreed standards for interoperability, security, and application-specific protocols.[13] Such a cross-industry standard would be a key step in establishing additional touchpoints for promoting and enforcing consistent security standards between ecosystem players, as well as ensuring supply chain integrity and overall security governance. For general data, the internationally recognized ISO 27001 specifies four security classes. Any cross-industry standard could start from this and include the specific challenges associated with machine-generated data outside the personal control of the user.[14]

Such a unified standard would also help consumers to better understand their risks and protections. They would be able to purchase end-point products from a range of suppliers knowing that a single trusted – and impartial – service provider oversees the necessary security and safety checks across devices.

Continuous and perpetual monitoring

Technical compliance alone, while vital, will hardly guarantee that security breaches never happen. An attack needs to be successful only once to inflict maximum damage to data security – and, crucially, to trust and reputation. The Future Home's cybersecurity must be effective continuously at all times.

To assume that anti-virus software alone can shield consumers from attacks and data leaks is a mistake. Nor can infrequent over-the-air software patches provide enough protection for the Future Home to weather cybercrime's increasing sophistication. The growing interoperability of devices opens up many new vulnerabilities. One compromised connected home product may enable another connected device in the household to go rogue.

Industry-wide agreed physical security features, wired into new connected devices, certainly help to stave off many dangers. Such device architectures must be built along agile design lines in which software components can be evolved after a device is deployed in a home. But beyond this, the Future Home in 5G must also introduce a continuous and perpetual monitoring mechanism for its devices and services. Such monitoring will also ensure that there is clear responsibility adopted by an individual player for when a specific product or service becomes a threat. In such an event a direct line of communication to the consumer – and ideally the device – is needed, and it must be possible to give support on the spot. This requires devices to be remotely adaptable so that the threat can be ring-fenced and neutralized.

Can there be a service product called Security-as-a-Service? The answer is yes. Accenture research shows that around 80 per cent of consumers prefer a single provider for all their digital needs,[15] indicating their propensity to trust a provider also for managed security services.

But to be attractive, such a provider will need to have an advanced security profile that continuously evolves to meet the ever-higher cybersecurity risks. This means permanently renewed approaches to advanced attack and readiness operations, to cyber operations and resilience, to application security, to cyber threat intelligence, and to incident response and threat hunting. What is more, such a provider must lean on new encryption technologies where data ledgers are stored across distributed servers, so that the most accurate and up-to-date record of transactions is maintained.

Such services could also entail cybersecurity education. Beyond device and data protection, service providers after all need to ensure their customers have the right awareness level of the security threats they face in the Future Home and know how to mitigate them. Service providers can develop and incorporate tutoring services, enabling customers to easily understand what to do and not do online, increasing their knowledge, for instance, of phishing or social engineering scams, letting them know what to look out for and how to act when suspicious activity is detected.

Furthermore, providers can tailor these services for both adults and younger consumers, based on their different usage patterns, level of innate trust in digital devices, and the propensity of younger generations to engage in higher-risk online behaviour such as video streaming through non-secure websites, storing passwords and login details online, and opening social media accounts.

Sowing customer trust and loyalty among the young

While many of us can still remember the advent of the internet – as we outline in the opening chapters, younger generations have been raised in the digital world, becoming tech-savvy from an early age, and adopting digital channels and devices for a multitude of experiences. Embracing a

DIFM attitude, this generation also has a higher propensity to leverage these channels to procure services that augment their day-to-day lives.

The younger generation has a stronger propensity to place their trust in a brand during the initial engagement phase. However, even loyalty leaders – including major disruptor brands – can't afford to rest on their laurels, as customer defection can be just a data breach or service experience failure away. Conversely, however, where another provider can step in to remedy the situation, the younger generation will have a higher level of attachment to this second brand, becoming fiercely loyal, and often vocal advocates. Millennials and Gen Z are accustomed to paying CSPs for services like wireless connectivity or home broadband on a monthly cadence. Hence they do not expect CSPs to sell their data as part of the core business model. We can see here that the CSPs' core business model is a good start to building up customer trust and loyalty among the young.

CSPs' strong starting point on data safety

The platform providers deserve to be highlighted in this chapter because they stand a good chance of snatching away the end-customer relationship from CSPs before they even get a hold of it. Through eSIM, for instance, a technology we introduced in Chapter 4, users could be free to choose their connectivity provider if industry players agree and, as a result, make it harder for CSPs to retain their direct customer relationships. In any event, this new technology is likely to phase in a new switching mentality, with one third of consumers already aware of eSIMs and 68 per cent interested in using them.[16]

But CSPs have a strong hand to play. As we have noted, their trump cards are incumbent consumer trust and a hitherto very high data privacy and data security record. We will explain in more detail in the next chapter how CSPs could leverage their capabilities to act as the orchestrator of the Future Home. As we noted in Chapter 2, 71 per cent of respondents in an Accenture survey said they would choose their CSP as the main provider of connected home services.[17] We have also already mentioned that CSPs can and should also bank on their longstanding billing relationships, using advanced analytics on their internal systems to generate insight regarding individuals within households as the basis for excellent hyper-personal services.

In current practice, connected home ecosystem players are often managing uncharted technology processes where every connected device has a potential vulnerability due to point-to-point connections and varying connectivity standards.[18] 5G, in contrast, will work like a uniform connectivity tissue in the home, allowing for consolidation of multiple standards into one, reducing security risks significantly. With one foot already in the door and by providing 5G networks and their new technology opportunities, CSPs could offer convenient support across all digital needs in the Future Home. This would crucially involve making sure that users only access home devices and services that offer a maximum of data privacy and data security.

Takeaways

1 At today's technology levels, a bad actor wanting to gain access to current connected homes has a high chance of success.

2 The Future Home industry and users need to have a clear position on standards for securing the storage and management of personal data, with users having first-hand control.

3 CSPs have a strong hand to play, with an advantage being incumbent consumer trust and a hitherto very high data privacy and data security record.

6

The rise of the connected living ecosystem builder

CHAPTER SUMMARY

....

Communications service providers (CSPs), whether they today deliver fixed-line or wireless connectivity or both, will play an all-important role in the Future Home in the 5G era. The emergence of these new markets will make these businesses want to expand beyond the traditional, static provision of connectivity to households and businesses and entice them to dynamically monetize the opportunities offered by the emerging Future Home service world. Three key factors position CSP operators to take up the role of Future Home ecosystem architects, builders and operators: trust, customer experience, and the ability to deliver mission-critical infrastructure. But there are six critical overall areas where CSPs must transform their business set-up and value chain to deliver these new connected services and capabilities.

....

As we have described from the outset in this book, the Future Home will be the foundation and, as such, the beginning of truly connected living for individuals, with enormous consequences for human society. This era will see the boundaries of the traditional brick-and-mortar home expand way beyond traditional physical walls. To deliver on this hyperconnected living experience through the Future Home, a broad-based ecosystem of partners and alliances must come together to reinvent, shape and design Future Home products and services, and to deliver the technologies, platforms and protocols that will make it a reality – whether based on conventional fixed-line broadband, cable, satellite, 5G wireless technologies or a heterogeneous combination.

The business opportunity is tremendous for CSPs. By 2023 the market for connected home services is poised to grow to $37.3 billion from around $20 billion today.[1] Much of this could be harvested by CSP players, as the data-powered experience they can offer to homes and businesses is without parallel in technology's history, meaning they should be well-prepared to offer unprecedented service quality.

A broad range of services – from intelligent home security and monitoring to remote healthcare, immersive entertainment and gaming and food delivery – can be reliably built on the basis of new homogenized technological standards, and give rise to swathes of new business cases. Once these different value pools are tapped, the momentum will continue. Service sophistication and personalization, enabled by enhanced data-driven insights and device control, will incessantly drive up the quality of Future Home services, orchestrated and, to a huge extent, monetized by CSPs as the main gatekeepers of connectivity to the Future Home.

This all sounds some distance away. And in fact, it is worth considering for a moment today's modest status quo of connected homes and services for this market. This will help us understand the giant business opportunity ahead.

In today's life, our home experience is driven by an only loosely orchestrated collection of 20 to 30 technology product and solution providers. Consumers have their individual choice of intelligent lighting solutions from utility providers, intelligent security through home solution providers, and intelligent devices and smart appliances from consumer electronics makers. For most of our in-home entertainment we engage with all sorts of sources offering linear broadcast, on-demand television, video streams, or gaming, also via various delivery methods. We have the choice of at least four to five different providers to meet each of these individual demands.

Then there is the multitude of platforms for connecting our different devices together, all positioning to become our home tech's central controlling hub, designed to be verticalized in their hardware, software, protocols and data.

In short, today's connected home is in most cases a wild array of self-contained solutions, a makeshift assemblage of atomized parts largely managed in ways that do not and cannot synch. This degree of fragmentation can't even be called a system let alone an ecosystem.

This status quo is holding back vendor businesses and the home tech markets overall. And it is only now, with an ever-increasing number of such point-to-point solutions in homes, that consumers and vendors likewise are becoming aware of this massively fragmented device and service reality. More and more people are longing for someone to navigate this jungle for them in true DIFM fashion.

The pressure for a guiding hand is rising by the day. The advance of hyper-connected home life and the invasion of sub-standard point-to-point use cases into homes will increase the size and complexity of this non-orchestrated solution jungle exponentially. This, in turn, will force the need for one or more players to take a leading role as orchestrators and principal builders who are able to support new products and services, facilitate the data flows between devices and fragmented hubs, and, in doing so, operationalize the Future Home as an unprecedented experience for 21st-century consumers. Underpinning this is the need to deliver these competencies in a seamless and centralized manner that empowers the end consumer to not only plug into new connected experiences easily, but to extract true user value and enrich their daily lives.

This raises two fundamental questions: Who is the ideal candidate to become the guiding hand? And what skillsets must be taken on board to become the Future Home's principal architect and lead orchestrator?

Who should be the guiding hand? Three reasons why CSPs are in pole position

Since wireless and fixed-line broadband are the foundations on which any connected service experience can be enabled, the CSPs that offer broadband connectivity in any form hold a prime position for unlocking the potential of truly intelligent future services and being the central enablers of an overall ecosystem.

Of course, other actors currently operating in today's disjointed connected home market could also take the lead. But we'd like to stress three things that make a strong case that CSPs are in pole position.

Old trust yields new trust

As outlined in the previous chapter, a fundamental requirement of the Future Home will be that its users trust it 100 per cent. The obligation is obvious in a situation where so many devices interconnect to share such unprecedented amounts of data about every aspect of our lives.

Currently, our personal data is only liberally regulated. It is often shared without our approval or even awareness, legally or via illegal hacks or data leaks, with third parties, authorities or the general public. CSPs stand out in this context for their strong data privacy standards, though they are not infallible.

This solid record gives them one of the highest trust scores of all service or product providers for connected homes. In some countries, home broadband invoices serve as trusted proofs of residential address when other data- and identity-sensitive items such as bank accounts are being dealt with. No wonder then that in a 2019 Accenture consumer survey,[2] fixed-line and wireless phone service providers ranked second and third, just behind banks, when it came to trust. Other parties likely to play a role in the Future Home rank significantly lower – for instance social media, search engine or digital voice assistant brands.

The increase in interconnectivity in our lives ushers in a new era of heightened responsibility to manage and work with our personal information in a perfectly secure and trustworthy manner. It is a responsibility not heeded by all data-using providers, as the numerous data privacy scandals of recent years demonstrate. The positive exception is the CSP sector, which benefits from the simple rule that those who can keep trust will be granted more trust in the future. As noted in Chapter 2 for instance, 49 per cent of Millennials would be prepared to choose their CSP for delivery of their home healthcare.[3]

Customer care experience

Earlier in the book we identified eight user mindsets that require different levels of customer experience and service profiles. The second consideration is therefore the need for CSP players to combine their exclusive operational knowhow, workforce, and capabilities to deliver a consistent, world-class customer experience in the Future Home. A successful customer experience will personalize the customer journey from start to finish, from bricks-and-mortar shop to serve to support. That means a cross-platform all-digital portal, operable with just minimal clicks during the shop and buy process. That means strategically located stores that can teach and demonstrate new Future Home services as well as serve as strategic supply chain distribution hubs to enable same-day delivery options for digital orders. It also means available and multi-disciplinary field force capabilities that can deliver orders, install complex solutions or provide white-glove set-ups. It furthermore means simplified ordering, activation and provisioning, demanding that CSPs build operational centres to answer and resolve user complaints in near real time – be it through social media, chatbots or agile engineer squads. The guiding principle should be: *solve problems before they happen* – for instance through data-analytics-enabled failure prediction.

CSPs can point to a rich legacy of expertise and capability in running large operational teams dealing with the complex experiences of numerous customers. In that regard their maturity is on a par with their level of trust – and far higher than that of other likely participants in the Future Home ecosystem.

Those other participants, such as the platform providers or device manufacturers, have often built cutting-edge capabilities in technology and solutions. Often having started up in the digital age, they may have a distinct edge in creating sophisticated digital products and services with excellent customer experience. But they still, crucially, lack the expertise and competency to manage the Future Home ecosystem over time and deal with all the nitty-gritty hiccups that hundreds of thousands of customers may want to see addressed within minutes.

This is the responsibility that will come with being the orchestrator: handling all the customer queries and complaints related to every aspect of the ecosystem. Whether it's an intelligent lighting solution in an individual household gone dark or the failure of some data handover between a car and a home or a hotel room, the orchestrator's success will depend on being able to fix it almost instantly.

The upside of this massive responsibility will be the ability to cash in on a large chunk of the joint ecosystem margin. Plus, as the gatekeepers and lead orchestrators of the Future Home ecosystem, orchestrators will have the responsibility to build partnerships using mutually beneficial business models with those involved.

To deliver all this successfully requires a distinct and difficult-to-replicate set of core competencies and workforce skills. Such competencies have always been inherent to the CSPs.

Mission-critical infrastructure

The third consideration is the CSPs' crucial role as controllers of access technology in the home. They are the exclusive providers of connectivity that links up homes, people, devices, autonomous vehicles, and society. Any one of us knows how vital this is, even if we mostly only fully realize it when a service goes down and life comes to a grinding halt.

So CSPs' qualification for orchestration and leadership is clear here. Without them, the Future Home wouldn't be possible. They provide the basis – the internet – the life-supporting communication between us, our devices and the services that run on them, without all of which a connected living experience simply couldn't happen. In that sense, it is almost an obligation for CSPs to take up the role of the Future Home ecosystem orchestrator.

Finally, we should bear in mind that this group of businesses is publicly regulated for a reason. Regulators not only focus on securing competition in the sector but aim to secure connectivity for the general public day and night, ensuring it is as reliable as hospitals or roads. CSP companies are forced by the authorities to keep infrastructure going and in good service. Their reliability, in other words, is double-sealed, mandated not just by markets, but by governments.

The market will continue to push and consumers will keep saying, 'I want someone to solve my fragmentation problem at home'. If no CSP jumps in, other digital giants could likely go to the regulator and ask to sell connectivity to Future Homes instead. The day this happens the sector will have missed a huge opportunity.

Breaking up the CSP value chain to unlock the Future Home: Six areas and six imperatives

So how should CSPs enable the connected services and capabilities that we have been describing?

The answer is that these businesses will have no option but to reinvent and reinvigorate their entire value chain. This wholesale reinvention and pivoting of structures and processes is the critical success factor.

Accenture has deeply analysed the CSP value chain, including the current approach to developing and distributing products and services, the aftermarket activity, and the way products and services are delivered to, operated by and maintained for end users. Based on this analysis, we have identified six areas that we believe form the blueprint for operators to successfully enable and monetize connected living experiences in the Future Home.

One: Reinvent the front office digitally

The front office, the layer through which CSPs interact with their customers, for example via browser-based or smartphone portals, represents much more than just a digital layer through which operators service their customers. To meet the Future Home's new customer environment head-on, every interaction between CSP and customer must become real-time and proactive, whilst giving customers a sense of control.

The shift is partly driven by the level of future interaction frequencies between consumer and CSP, which is forecast to increase over the coming years. It is particularly necessary in the light of the rise of the 'liquid' customer who, increasingly impatient, is prepared to switch to a comparable offering the moment the service disappoints or seems unresponsive.

At a more practical level, in orchestrating the Future Home, the front office's primary function will be to unlock a pervasive set of excellent Future Home experiences for customers in near real time. Customer interfaces therefore need drastic revamps. They must become powerful two-way communication dashboards that can phase services in and out quickly across all types and sophistication levels, from intelligent thermostats to the automatic replacement of fridge contents to immersive conference technology for business meetings at home and in the autonomous vehicle – the whole range of Future Home technology users want to have around them.

It is clear that such a dashboard does not yet exist, but given the enormous business opportunities, it is a prime imperative for any CSP. From a purely technical perspective, the reinvention of CSP front offices will unlock a gateway through which customers can engage with their provider on their own terms. This requires CSPs to build, run and maintain an augmented customer experience layer that is AI-powered and driven by data intelligence. Building such a layer is a fundamental departure from the traditional customer relationship management and business support systems layers that operators have built and maintained over decades.

The change is necessary because in the Future Home, CSPs must cater for each customer individually – even as the client count goes into the millions. Automation, including automated customer care through things like chatbots, is the only way to do it. To give a practical example, for Swisscom,[4] Accenture has implemented a digital omni-channel platform (DOCP) which is designed to accelerate its ability to offer an omnichannel experience across all lines of customer interaction – via online, in-store, call centres, mobile apps and social channels.

Two: Reinvent the back office

As already implied by our discussion of new capabilities and technologies at CSPs' front offices, this must go hand in hand with the reinvention of technologies, structures and processes in the back office – ie everything that will ultimately deal with management of Future Home networks and the concomitant data flows.

Many CSPs still have siloed, inflexible, old-style operational support systems. The back office must instead become as agile and responsive as the business now aims to be for customers; a pervasive and active co-worker with the front office. Accordingly, operational management and the creation and operationalization of aftermarket customer processes will be fundamental, as will having the tools and techniques to partner with and support human interaction. Without these, the scale of customer retention required to operationalize connected businesses will be impossible.

A practical move towards all this would be for CSPs to migrate to intelligent network operations. These are automated systems making heavy use of AI to anticipate consumer and/or internal staff expectations and needs and thereby provide seamless experiences enabling CSPs to transform their traditional operating model into a digital platform organization that delivers better value to customers. These would be able to manage the implementation of new capabilities, establishing a path to becoming the central service provider within ecosystems.

Back-office operations would become lean and agile, supporting the innovative, dynamic business models required and their high-frequency customer interactions.

Take the example of robotic process automation engines operating as part of such a solution. Get ready for the science bit: they can automatically open issue tickets, note that a customer problem has been registered and is being dealt with, and execute diagnostics as well as doing customer impact analysis and dispatching tickets until closure. An algorithmic digibot awakens with an alarm and completes diagnostic checks and automatically fills the impacted customers into the customer relationship management system.

If all this is Greek to you, here's a nice instance of how such an engine works in practice. At US telecommunications company CenturyLink, an AI agent named Angie works with sales managers to identify the most promising sales leads. Intelligent Angie engages with leads via email and interprets the interactions to determine which ones to drop or pursue. The solution generates 40 hot leads for sales managers each month and so far has earned US $20 in new contracts for every dollar spent on the system.[5]

Or consider Spanish CSP Telefónica as a role model example for using such novel technology set-ups. In a selection of its markets, the company has deployed an AI-based cognitive assistant called Aura that is activated by customer voices. The permanent verbal input triggers the system to learn constantly and this type of interaction allows Aura to eventually come up with strongly personalized recommendations for support. The use of such technology not only leads to massively improved customer experience levels – it also renders internal processes much more efficient as algorithms work with higher precision and without time limits, compared to human operators.[6] Aura-generated findings also help to improve predictive maintenance and network optimization.

The business of being a CSP, as you can see, is rendered much more customer-centric. End-to-end execution of large network programs across complex delivery ecosystems is scaled and orchestrated by anticipating consumer expectations and providing seamless experiences.

Three: Train and equip your talent for the future CSP

The glue that will bind the new agile organization is your people and talent – a notion that is routinely emphasized but not fully realized in reality. This cannot be the case any longer. CSPs will require a very different workforce landscape to secure their role as ecosystem builder in the emerging Future Home markets. Fortunately, CSP business leaders seem to understand that digital technologies have redefined the way people work and that they must act accordingly.

As a central example of what's driving the change, take AI, currently propelling the CSP workforce to the next level of digital transformation. It is worth discussing in some detail because, even as only one of the key technologies, it represents such extensive systematic change. It is now not just about augmenting the tasks staff members and service personnel carry out but accelerating the pace of organizational change and value creation. Ericsson has, for instance, automated 400,000 hours of work per year, using over 100 robotic process automation bots, which have processed over a million transactions. The telecoms equipment maker has thereby witnessed cost, quality, customer satisfaction and lead time improvements across functions and business areas.[7]

AI can also hugely enhance employee and customer experiences, enable agility, collaboration and personalization, and speed up decision making. For CSPs, AI can also usher in new jobs and opportunities that allow intelligent workforces to shine. In fact, 63 per cent of CSP leaders expect intelligent technologies to generate net job gains in the next three years. CSP workers are excited by the possibilities and ready for change; 82 per cent are confident about working with intelligent technologies.[8]

But consider today's reality with regard to skills. The average age of the CSP workforce is mid to late forties. To unlock the skills and talent of the future, organizations will need to undergo considerable rotation of their workforce. More experienced workers will remain valuable for their wisdom and experience, but more digitally savvy generations will also be needed.

CSP businesses will need, specifically, these workers to provide a competitive set of competencies, including infrastructure, telecommunications, software, design, service design and design thinking skills, all handled in such a way as to put user experience at the heart of every process and customer interaction.

This talent does not freely exist in the market today, nor is it emerging directly from universities. Instead, providers will need to nurture these skills over the coming years to develop the workforce they need. CSPs will effectively have to create internal academies providing tailored training schemes for their respective business units.

Four: Kick-start rapid-fire product development

Creating a new product and service development layer within a traditional CSP organization is easier said than done. For the Future Home markets, a mindset shift is required to launch services in just weeks or in some cases only days. Bear in mind that today's CSP products are often entrenched in development and testing cycles lasting months if not years. As the gatekeepers, CSPs should seek to become the quickest and most innovative pacemakers in their ecosystem. This is not only a matter of pride; it is operationally necessary as CSPs will not only be offering their own products to consumers but also delivering those of their ecosystem partners. They cannot afford to become a bottleneck. And they cannot fall short of the promise they give to their customers – on each individual service, but also, and even more importantly, around privacy, security and ethical AI. Evolution of technological capabilities in these areas is so fast that CSPs need to completely reinvent their way of working to keep up with what is going on around them.

To achieve the necessary speed, CSPs will need to move to agile development based on data gathered from usage, collaborating with end users – customers – and creating a trust-based relationship where the client base, in tandem with ecosystem partners, support product testing and development. They will have to do this even without a fully developed business case or clear expectation of success and return on investment. Customers and their preferences will dictate innovation cycles through direct response to CSPs – often in real time – and offerings developed to meet specific needs may have to be sunsetted faster than they were developed as new customer requirements emerge. Monetization will shift to after launch. Instead of CSPs selling a service and its infrastructure upfront, they will charge based on individual customer outcomes.

This rapid-fire product development culture is closer to the classic 'fail fast' start-up mentality than the diligent market receptibility assessments prior to launch that are typical for sector incumbents.

If done well, the new monetization model will become a key feature of the Future Home for all players, with customers billed for the individual offerings they purchase, allowing each to have the most tailored and personalized experience possible. All this will depend on the speed, responsiveness, and agility we have just described.

Five: Revamp your technology platforms

A similarly rapid and radical change is needed in CSPs' technology platforms. To successfully scale new businesses, they will need open platforms that connect consumers and suppliers and deliver 'as a service'.

Platforms are different from traditional models in two key ways: they can scale at unprecedented rates, mainly driven by the low cost of customer acquisition, and by network effects. And they allow businesses to accelerate innovation and develop features at a pace that is only possible because they are not operating alone, but are able to continuously absorb and seamlessly integrate an ever-expanding universe of Future Home ecosystem partner constituents.

As we have said, the Future Home ecosystem will need to add new devices and services seamlessly, growing with customer needs and the rapid technological evolution. A CSP running the platform could assure that devices are tested for security and ease of use. And by combining their consumer data analytics and a digital hub, then leveraging an ecosystem of providers for commerce, CSPs can also offer a personalized service marketplace.

But by definition these platforms will also need to be multi-vendor and open source, enabling a platform that can absorb and co-create with a multitude of ecosystem constituents that is set to increase over time. With the innovation cycle accelerating and technologies depreciating and evolving much faster, agility is also key here, requiring platforms that are open, fully virtualized and API-driven, featuring programmable interfaces that can work across standards and partners and create best-of-breed multi-vendor solutions.

Creating such service-driven solutions will also require a mindset shift in the way technology platforms are built. CSPs have already started to move away from the traditional, highly structured and hierarchical waterfall model to the agile, DevOps-inspired culture we discussed in Area Four above – but their focus and application need to accelerate, and must be embraced end-to-end across networks, systems, processes and people, and not just at the IT layer. And they need to have a super-crisp architectural vision and execution capability that allows them to design these new platforms to be secure and responsible and to respect the highest privacy standards by design.

If done correctly, the lines will indeed blur between the ways in which software and communications platforms are built, unlocking a new layer of convergence critical to the realization of the connected living experience.

Six: Activate a pervasive connectivity layer

We described in Chapter 4 how orchestrating the Future Home would require deploying 5G along with a set of complementary technologies such as eSIM, edge computing and advanced analytics. The final and arguably most important pillar of this transformation is to embed a pervasive connectivity layer that binds all the other elements together and provides the ubiquitous connectivity required to power the connected home.[9] As we have stated from the start of this book, 5G – with its speed, scale and low latency – is the binding force that can deliver the Future Home's scalable connected living.

But to build the Future Home in 5G, a paradigm shift is also required in the way CSPs approach connectivity. Accenture has identified four actions that we believe are critical:

1 Building intelligent network operations, as discussed under Area Two: Reinvent the back office.

2 Establishing a layer of programmable network platforms that fit into the overarching platform capability.

3 Unlocking network services in a way that enables them to be consumed by higher layers of services.

4 Creating on-demand infrastructures in the home that are elastic and have the capacity to absorb new services – requiring new bandwidth, cost optimization and monetization models, and a renewed outlook on network economics.

CSPs need to maintain their current strong positions as well as future proof against the disruptive threats of other kinds of business looking to take a central role in the Future Home market. Yet, as much we have said here indicates: the newly acquired security will be one in which scaling to new growth will be a deliberate and perpetual journey of change. It will not be a single transformative event.

As the pace of change and technology innovation increases, and we embrace the notion that the 5G-enabled Future Home will follow us wherever we go, consumers will progressively increase their level of comfort with this connectivity layer. As they do, their perception of it will shift too, morphing from today's notion of connectivity as a 'hygiene factor' – necessary to ward off dissatisfaction, but not particularly satisfying – into one that not only unlocks experiences that make us feel at home regardless of where we are, but also enriches the experience overall.

Figure 6.1   Breaking up the CSP value chain to unlock the Future
Home – six imperatives

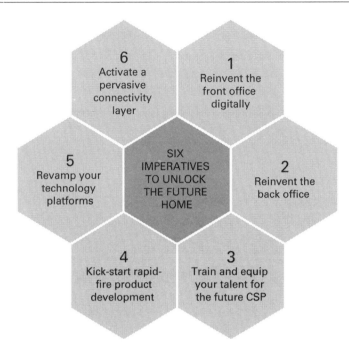

By getting this right, CSPs will create a very sticky customer experience
that builds loyalty – vital in light of today's disruptive market dynamics
and fickle customer behaviour.

Takeaways

1 CSP businesses enjoy a head start in the race for the Future Home
as they combine high consumer trust with close customer
relationships and gatekeeping connectivity infrastructure.

2 But the CSP sector needs to revamp its approach, digitize its front
and back offices, train talent for the new service world and adopt
quicker product development cycles.

3 It is paramount for CSPs to build agile platform businesses that can
accommodate ecosystems involving a wide array of partners.

7

Emerging business models for the Future Home

CHAPTER SUMMARY

....

In order to make the most of the emerging Future Home market, communications service providers (CSPs) will need to evolve their incumbent vertically integrated service provider model. To stay relevant in the digital daily routines of their customers, they will set themselves up as a multi-sided platform orchestrating and coordinating the Future Home. The move represents huge opportunities as it means controlling data and its flows rather than just being an infrastructure provider supplying connectivity. As a whole new business model this is faster, much more nimble and expansive than the old one. It requires a very different set-up, not just internally, but with various external stakeholders: tech specialists in device manufacturing, app development, AI capability and edge computing, and also a wider range of service providers from non-tech sectors such as health, finance or entertainment to name just a few. These partners must find a mode of alliance that rewards all their contributions to the multi-sided platform effort – with CSPs having the best chances of becoming the main orchestrators.

....

The Future Home will be built around a new value chain of ecosystem partners. Opportunities around this newly emerging market will invite those partners to benefit and extract enormous value. Everybody joining the value chain will need to develop initiatives to contribute in some form or another to Future Home solutions with outstanding user experience – in areas such as streaming multi-player gaming, energy management, remote home health or immersive entertainment. Flexible and organically morphing partnerships will evolve, enabling CSPs to undertake entirely new operational approaches behind novel business models.

The limited return for CSPs of conventional home services

Against this rather fluid future scenario, most of today's incumbent CSPs have tried to remain the equivalent of static soloists rather than orchestra conductors with a talent for improvization. Their main aim was, and in most cases still is, to sell bundles of handpicked connected home services at most, and connected devices alone in some cases, to the millions of customers they cater for as legacy infrastructure providers connecting households to broadband networks. This strategy has not been without success, as solutions such as Xfinity Home from Comcast or Magenta Smart Home from Deutsche Telekom demonstrate, though the question remains if such business models could not get a further economic boost by being tweaked towards a broader alliance model.

In Chapter 4, we discussed the issues with today's connected home. To recap, it starts with a hub, a central hardware item in the home that is equipped to handle different radio standards, functioning as a universal connector for various devices. Applications running on the devices allow users to control and derive data from them, managing things like energy usage or the video from the connected doorbell. None of this, however, has really delivered relevant growth or significant new profit pools for CSPs or other companies active in the field. While there is admittedly some value in managing energy consumption, controlling lighting, or looking after the house when you are away, the benefits for users and providers alike are so far limited because each service only works in isolation.

Some incumbent CSPs have introduced a service fee for cellular connected devices in the home to recover the investment and increase their average revenue per user (ARPU). This, however, has not been convincingly successful either. Even among those customers paying the fee, only a few have really activated the cellular and used the service. This is rather a risk, as it does not deliver on the promise CSPs charge their customers for every month, and it could turn into reputational damage for their entire franchise if customers find out that they have paid without getting significant benefits in return. So, it is hard to see how CSPs can drive a significant connected-home business profitably within their traditional business models.

Voice-controlled platform devices: Leading the way to the Future Home

At the same time, when CSPs started promoting their proprietary home offerings, the first voice-enabled ambient devices such as Amazon Alexa or Google Home entered the market, putting a smart device on people's coffee tables or mantelpieces: the personal home assistant. Though many users had concerns about trust and privacy vis-a-vis such speaker devices, millions of households have adopted them in just a few years.

The devices crucially boast voice control, which significantly increases their usability. However, even more importantly, they focus not on connecting devices in the home but on solving a two-sided problem: for the user, they provide interesting and relevant use cases wrapped in a customer experience that most people like; at the same time, third parties can add skills to such assistant devices, so that the range of services can grow steadily. Incumbent CSPs have also entered this new market. In a joint big push, Orange and Deutsche Telekom have created their own version of a voice-enabled assistant. Its main difference from pioneering precursors is a promise to handle personal data differently, with an offering specifically designed around security and privacy.[1] Concurrently, this CSP-provided assistant still works to the same basic model as the devices that led the way: an open, multi-sided platform approach.

How multi-sided platforms will disrupt vertical integration

With this notable exception, the traditional CSP approach to business remains, as we have said, that of a siloed vertically integrated service provider. We say it's time for them to take heed of Amazon and Google's success with a platform model and try to understand how they can harvest the benefits themselves, or team up with an existing platform and tweak it in a way that it creates a credible benefit for their end user. The opportunity is big and the crucial open question is whether CSPs can seize it and thereby put themselves at the profitable centre of Future Home markets.

Why is now the moment for CSPs to seriously consider transitioning from vertically integrated service provider to multi-sided platforms? There's a strong argument that vertical integration was always vulnerable to disruption. CSP incumbents have a long history of adding services to their main role of infrastructure access providers. In the early days, they introduced portals and access to exclusive content to foster loyalty, reduce customer churn and escape pricing pressure in competitive markets. However, that led to several waves of 'walled garden' building where CSPs offered their own proprietary services and remained inward looking, making little effort to partner with or platform other service providers' offerings. In most cases, this created limited economic value, even though it helped stabilize market share for a while.

But recent communications tech history provides multiple warnings against vertical integration long-term. Because eventually a platform will appear and disrupt your business. Take mobile telco portals like i-mode, Terra or T-Online. They have been eclipsed, first by Google Search on the computer, and then by Android on the smartphone. Google saw that, with Android, it could be both the provider of a mobile telecommunications and internet operating system, offering a platform for third-party apps. Profit for them came both from these collaborations directly and from the value they added to customers – without owning or over-curating one single bit of content delivered over the platform.[2]

The 5G wireless standard likely provides an additional discontinuity threat to the integrated business model for CSPs. While traditionally asset-oriented financial investment in the physical network has been the key source of revenue for incumbents – and their exclusive defendable control points – the physical assets are increasingly being superseded in importance by data flows and software. After all, 5G networks bring the great novelty of very low latency, high speed and broad data capacity, connecting devices directly to one network. Such capabilities can consolidate access and data traffic from a Future Home into one single wireless transmission channel. And this crucially allows home services and home devices to rely more on configurable software, with the immediate effect that services reach a much higher quality and become more deeply involved into the lives of home consumers. CSPs can be at the heart of this, if they contribute the essential elements that will make the Future Home work – relevance, scalability, experience and trust.

Seeking service relevance for the end user within ecosystems

To create true economic value for themselves and sufficient user value for the consumer, CSPs will have to increase their relevance in the daily digital routines of Future Home users. In order to accomplish this, they need to find ways to open up and engage with some form of ecosystem. And that entails not least reinventing the new front-office and back-office capabilities, and all the innovative skillsets and capabilities laid out in the previous chapter. CSPs taking up this challenge will become orchestrators of ecosystems for their customers and users.

The departure from their traditional integrated business model is massive though, the success factors and critical capabilities in a platform and ecosystem-based market being significantly different. The following list (Figure 7.1) provides an overview of how far apart these two business models are. One can see from it how drastically the capital expenditure, the key performance indicators (KPIs) and the creation of good consumer experiences shifts. From their old siloed, vertical, in-house structures, CSPs must take responsibility for a whole Future Home ecosystem which safeguards the data flow and provides not only services to the user, but also a broad suite of ancillary services to the ecosystem.

Figure 7.1 From the old to the new for CSPs: Vertical integration vs platform ecosystems

		VERTICALLY INTEGRATED SERVICE PROVIDER	ECOSYSTEM PLATFORM PLAYER
	Control points	Contract, physical control points, customer service	Manage identity, security and privacy as well as data stocks and flows
	KPIs	ARPU	Reach
	Business focus	Bundling services	Relevance and ecosystem around tradeable information and data
	Customer engagement	Minimize interaction	Open and seamless omnichannel experience
	Go to market	Own and third-party channels	Federated through ecosystem
	Investment profile	80+% network infrastructure assets	Software capabilities Leverage ecosystem for infrastructure investments
	Products and services	Communication services and bundling content	Enabling ecosystem-based services
	Platform	Walled garden-based Closed	Ecosystem-based Open
	Talent management	Own the full delivery chain and vendor management	Owning the experience and heavy leverage of ecosystem skills

Conquering new control points as a data gatekeeper

In the five years since Alexa was first introduced in November 2014, Amazon has sold more than 100 million such devices. More than 100,000 Alexa skills have been developed by third parties as of today, and 150–200 skills are added each day. Amazon attracted a developer community that is now in the hundreds of thousands.[3] CSPs can find similar success, but, in another crucial departure from their incumbent business model, they will need to find a way to master the massive scalability challenge with the developer community.

In order to do so, CSPs will again find orientation in the success of dominant smartphone operating systems such as Android. It attracts a huge developer community that contributes new applications constantly and similar activity is currently observable around the voice-enabled platforms we just discussed.

In this new approach, data control points will be on connected devices – routers and set-top-boxes as well as voice-enabled devices. And as 5G wireless networks play a greater role in the Future Home, further data control points will evolve directly from this CSP-owned network. So CSPs must find ways to access and control the data flows, and manage them on behalf of the customer. We recommend that CSPs differentiate themselves with notions of trust, safety, reliability and security – because the new role of such providers will entail being principal managers of protected customer data, the information that flows from the various third-party devices in the Future Home.

The more data control points there are, the more user transactions a platform owner can enable within their ecosystem, and that means more value for them.

Figure 7.2 shows the various chambers of value CSPs could tap, grouped around their core service of delivering 5G connectivity to homes.

One can see on the chart that CSPs have a broad set of control points under their aegis from which to extract relevant user data. They have the billing relationship with millions of end customers. They run the physical

Figure 7.2 Potential data control points in a CSP's platform ecosystem

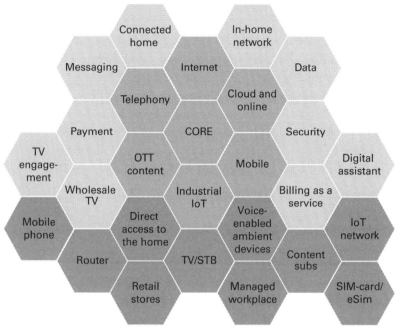

▬ Physical control points
▬ Core services
▬ Service based control points

access point in the home in the shape of routers or set-top boxes. They own the SIM cards built into devices. They already have access to some connected devices on the edge of the networks and are adding new control points there as they move into 5G.

Justifying data control through excellent user experience

The main challenge of such a strategy might be that CSPs are not always allowed to use the data flows running through their networks and turn them into tradable assets with the trusted Future Home ecosystem partners. To become authorized to use them in line with customer expectations, they need, simply, to provide excellent and essential service. The user's net benefit from a Future Home service needs to be higher than the perceived loss of control over specific personal or usage data.

Yes, CSPs also need to prove that they won't abuse their controlling power over user data. But privacy and security pledges are not enough without great customer experience. Numerous research studies have shown how much value users attach to good experiences of services and products. They deepen consumer trust and the inclination to sustain a relationship with a service provider. The explosion of internet services and mobile applications outside the Future Home is the proof: consumers are happy to share data if they can trade it for a service that creates true value for them.

Customers trust services that they find relevant and helpful in their daily routines. One CSP, Swisscom, recently introduced a new omni-channel platform (OCE, Omnichannel Customer Experience), the primary focus of which is no longer the product but its user.[4] The platform gives Swisscom a view on each of their customers, making it possible for the first time for them to understand which service is consumed by which user in any given household. In March 2019, Telia of Sweden launched Telia Smart Family, a concept in which a CSP proactively supports their household communities' daily digital routines.[5] For most CSPs, however, achieving this kind of relevance to customers is still a long and ongoing journey. And even the ones who have adopted platform technology, like the above examples, are still at the beginning of their journey to turn the newly acquired capabilities into real new value for their customers.

The platform need for partnerships and alliances

In the past, CSPs just integrated partner services into their products and offered the whole bundle under their name. Thus, the whole value chain hinged on the successful marketing of such bundles. The value that was generated, small as it was, was then distributed by the CSP to all contributing parties and the ecosystem was dependent on the CSP pulling the train.

In stark contrast, the Future Home must be dominated by open platforms that, unlike the bundle approach, offer incentives for all participants to build their own business case using the platform's capabilities. Many types of partners need to be attracted to build and sustain the platform's growth and success. It starts with connected devices and services. Instead of being integrated into bundled offers, they need to have the opportunity to provide their services either directly to the user or to offer the functionality and data that is generated to other applications.

Then there are all the different industry partners from areas like healthcare, fitness, finance, insurance, consumer goods, retail, food delivery and more. CSPs will need to attract all of them to join the platform over time.

Next comes the developer community. There are about 25 million developers active globally. Of those, 7.5 million work in Europe and Asia, a good 5 million are in North America, and the rest are distributed across the globe. Sixty-five per cent of them work part-time and nevertheless want to earn incremental money on their applications or see adoption of their great ideas.[6] They therefore only put their effort behind platforms that create sufficient reach.

Finally, other service providers will be needed. They'll support CSPs when it comes to unlocking edge computing, big data analytics, AI and machine-learning-based insight creation, actionable analytics, security services, and payment and delivery services.

To attract such partners, CSPs will need to offer platforms that have a value proposition superior to the conventional platforms already run by CSPs bundling media content via infrastructure products. The key to success will be finding the way to transition to the new, more attractive platform models without abandoning what is profitable about the old.

At the same time CSPs – often former state monopolies active within national borders – need to achieve scalability and reach if they want to appeal to developers. How, for instance, would a home service app developer in Singapore find a CSP in Canada worth partnering with on a Future Home solution when there is only a small market in Canada amounting to just 10 per cent of the population of the United States, and they, anyway, can only be reached via designated data protocols provided by a specific CSP?

International standards are the solution here. CSPs have seldom been very successful in collaborating to create globally scaling platform solutions or standards, but now it will be essential that they align themselves behind one or two global standards. Where they once did – for example when they agreed on the global GSM wireless standard – they created exponential value for both themselves as well as for users and society. They just need to do it again.

Why individual connected home apps are not enough

Most operators so far have tried to win the battle for the home with a home automation application. iControl by Comcast and Qivicon by Deutsche Telekom were early and successful attempts.[7] iControl had the advantage of providing a cheaper DIY-like home security solution than most of its alternatives. But from any perspective, the advantages of this approach had to be developed further.

As on a smartphone, so in the home: what's needed is not just one app that allows the user to steer a specific scenario, it's myriad little things that make life better and support us every day – as well as a continuous stream of innovation offered to the user by inventive developers.

In Chapter 2 we looked at eight different user mindsets and the proliferation of Future Home needs. It is unlikely that just one app will cater to all of these needs and keep the different user segments interested. CSPs can still offer their own applications, and they surely will. But at the same time they need to provide open application programming interfaces (APIs) for third parties to bring their own offerings to the household customers. This will be the route for CSPs to attaining multiple control points, generating data and turning that data into tradeable assets that deliver value for all – CSPs, ecosystem partners and consumers.

The protracted game of aligning platform partner incentives

All ecosystem partners will have different interests that CSPs will need to understand and align with. A key task here will be reinventing monetization so as to provide incentives for all partners to get involved.

While some device manufacturers may not expect any additional revenue streams to come from connecting their devices, only being interested in the relevance and attractiveness of their products in a Future Home, other industry partners may already be in a service business or on the path to turning their hardware business at least partially into one. As a consequence, some may want to create a broader service portfolio on their own, offering a stream of innovation-based services through their hardware to the household.

Developers will look for reach and for monetization opportunities as well as for the customer experience they can create on a specific platform. Service providers in turn will either look to sell opportunities to the CSP to enhance their platform capabilities or to work jointly with the CSP to sell value-added services to households, connected device manufacturers, or industry partners – things like services to enhance broadband coverage in the home, firewalls, and other security solutions, or specific services to enhance experience.

All these different partner types will judge their engagement based on the scalability and reach they can generate if they partner with CSPs. They will also assess the ease of creating incremental service revenues around a Future Home platform. These groups will be very much driven by reach and the convenience of creating a business around the CSP platform.

How basic services can attract new ecosystem partners

The appeal to third parties will also, crucially, be driven by the attractiveness and ease of use provided by the CSP service catalogue to the end user. That includes identity management, service discovery, value-added offerings around service delivery (notification, fulfilment, assurance, billing), and the opportunity for continuous learning and feedback from usage. Only if CSPs can keep up with industry best practice for these services will partners be loyal.

So CSPs as platform orchestrators can attract partners by offering a lot of basic services to them. Via their infrastructure control points, they can manage end-user identities when a third party wants to offer a service on the platform. Due to the rich user data assets they create from studying user behaviour, they can also suggest services to ecosystem partners and add components of service fulfillment, service assurance or service optimization for a service offered by a third party. Finally, they can provide ecosystem partners with user feedback.

While today CSPs mainly receive their revenue streams from subscription services for connectivity from the end-user, in the Future Home, all those ancillary services can create additional revenue streams and increasingly turn CSPs into very profitable ecosystem orchestrators.

Takeaways

1 The multi-sided platform is at the heart of the success of Amazon, and the hitherto vertically siloed CSPs need to grasp the benefits of such platforms.

2 Opening up, controlling and managing data, instead of infrastructure, will allow CSPs to create advanced Future Home data management services that hold higher margin value for themselves and trusted partners.

3 Any CSP remaining in its 'walled garden' should be under no illusion: it will have to change anyway, one way or another. CSPs need to become open ecosystem orchestrators building on relevance, scalability, experience and trust.

8

Creating incentives for the Future Home ecosystem

CHAPTER SUMMARY

For the Future Home in the 5G era and beyond to become a success with consumers, ambitious rebuilding is required from the industries involved. Various hurdles beyond technology fragmentation in the home stand in the way. One of the biggest is the persistent siloing of data that would need – in the interest of good user experiences – to flow unhindered between devices, service providers, hardware manufacturers and developers. As long as there is not enough incentive to break those closely controlled silos and get all ecosystem participants to feed into a joint data reservoir – while respecting the data rights of each individual contributor and the usage rights assigned – it is futile to try and pull off the Future Home. A solution could be to create a central data-handling body controlled by a neutral industry initiative.

The Future Home is only going to take off under certain conditions. One of the most important is that the home's resources – connected devices and services from industry partners – must create a sufficiently rich user experience. Only then will household members let such service offerings support the daily digital routines and individualized use cases connected to their Future Home.

In the current status quo, various hurdles make it difficult to get this job done, although incoming new technologies will lower these obstacles substantially. The phasing-in of 5G connectivity, with its low latency and high data transmission, will solve a lot of the issues – among them the legacy multitude of radio standards as well as isolated point-to-point set-ups for existing connected home devices. So 5G will foster the evolution of ecosystems around Future Home solutions, which will then help to reach a level of experience excellence that is accepted by consumers. Some CSPs will follow the examples already mentioned such as Comcast Xfinity and Telia Smart Family and put customer experience and a user-focused mindset at the centre of their offerings, bundling broadband infrastructure to media content. Xfinity, for instance, allows users to invite up to six other users to one account, making such an offering attractive to family homes. Others will go all the way in transforming themselves into platform operators – in the way we analysed in the previous chapter.

So what will such providers have to do to attract both customers and the necessary partners to make their platforms work?

The Future Home as pre-emptive multi-tasker

To work out the necessary ingredients of a Future Home platform's success, it will be helpful to start with an analysis of what such a hyper-connected home set-up must be able to deliver. The Future Home will support both the household community overall and individual users in their digital daily routines. Today's equivalent of a centralized command post for our day-to-day lives is the smartphone. In the future, our digital life management will become increasingly independent from individual devices. Instead, the Future Home will proactively steer us, both at home and on the move, via services that are unobtrusive but preemptive. The Future Home will be user-centric, context-aware, and will have the mandate of making recommendations and managing a broad range of services on our behalf.

Ideally it will understand user needs before they arise. It will have enough hardware and software-induced 'brain' on board to see what services and connected devices need to collaborate and how a desired outcome for a specific user can be created at any moment. That is, no doubt, a tall order and to achieve it the Future Home needs to be sufficiently intelligent to understand the wider context of user action and thinking, to learn from these human intents and moves and to be able to predict and confirm them.

Just consider how many different inter-device data communications are needed to make the following relatively simple home experience a seamless and helpful reality. A Future Home dweller needs to get to work on time in the morning – but he or she has overslept by half an hour. The Future Home's job as a competent life assistant will be to get its inhabitant to work on time possibly by dropping some routines completely and maybe speeding others up, or by finding quicker travel alternatives. Morning routines to be juggled by the Future Home will include using the bathroom, choosing attire for the day, getting the briefcase sorted, having breakfast, ordering a cab, planning the fastest route to work, and a whole raft of other tasks that could delay or expedite arrival time.

One can see right away that the Future Home ecosystem needs to solve a complex multitude of connected and otherwise unrelated problems all at once to get to a result that is really helpful. It needs, for instance, an understanding of what 'on time' actually means. Is it a fixed time, or is it the first meeting in the schedule of a user for a particular day? Furthermore, the Future Home needs to understand the calendar. It needs to know the different travel options and how to use them. And it crucially needs to be able to flow-optimize all the morning routines as a seamless ensemble.

Five properties for an effective Future Home

Translating such a coordinated chain of events and device functions into a convincing user experience is, to put it mildly, quite ambitious.

First, smooth and seamless connectivity to all kinds of devices and services is needed. 5G will help to improve connectivity and service discovery. But CSPs need to provide the entire catalogue of enabling services for the Future Home, as we said at the end of the last chapter. It is important to note that the Future Home won't only connect devices, it will also tie in existing external web services and applications and will need, in addition, to be able to manage application programming interfaces (APIs), standard communication protocols, from a multitude of services autonomously.

Second, the platform must be able to work out the context and meanings of user action and planning in order to be pre-emptive. To do this, it will need to know which services and connected devices can be helpful in interpreting user intent and routines. Such a system must be able to search the capabilities of many services and connected objects, and check on the contextual information available that would also influence their responses – such as traffic information that would influence the choice of travel mode. The Future Home will, in short, need to be able to undertake semantic searches across the universe of things surrounding the user.

Third, the Future Home needs elaborate AI and machine-learning-optimization power to make things really seamless. As we outlined in Chapters 5 and 6, the Future Home ecosystem will already have learned from experience to interpret intentions and adjust its recommendations based on contextual information. This will help it understand which morning routines are more important and which less – whether the first coffee is a must and whether the newspaper digest can perhaps be skipped and transferred into the autonomous vehicle to save time. The Future Home will be able to evaluate all these options and scenarios and come up with recommendations. It will adapt and move to a next best option if the user does not follow a specific recommendation.

Fourth, the Future Home must have authority over user identification and authentication as well as payments of all sorts. As already outlined, data privacy and security must be one of the cornerstones of any successful Future Home strategy, so the platform driving it will need to have secure access to all connected devices and services used in the home. It must be able to identify and authenticate all users individually using knowledge it has accumulated over time or from preset user profiles. It must even have authority to pay in their name, for example when a smart fridge autonomously orders new dairy products for the week. In order to do all this, the Future Home needs to be able to access all these sources of information, which requires watertight data privacy, safety, ethics and security management. No data must be released that the user would not want to share. It also means that documenting controls need to be in place – for example, provided by distributed ledger and blockchain technologies – so that no data is used outside the context for which it is needed.

The fifth challenge Future Home ecosystems will need to master is closely related to number four: within its ecosystem, a great number of autonomous decisions on access and execution of services will be taken on behalf of the user. This will only be acceptable if the user can fully trust these system actions. He or she needs to be able to independently set the platform's role concept, access and usage rights, and overrule decisions at any point in time.

How data silos kill viable ecosystems and good user experience

The important point here remains that all the data needed to handle the tasks and obligations described in our five points is buried in silos today. As it currently stands, the Future Home platform would have no chance of accessing even the coffee machine, let alone giving recommendations on the mobile phone or other screens, or steering devices to do the right thing – such as calling ride-sharing services, opening a music playlist, or checking tomorrow's work schedule. Persistent data siloing also means it wouldn't understand much context, as it has never been exposed to such complex scenarios. This would mean it would not be able to give recommendations for action.

Even worse, many of the potential ecosystem partners that need to work together for this scenario would think twice if asked to commit data outside their current silo. They would first ask what's in it for them in terms of sufficient monetizable user experience guaranteed by viable business cases for them. Only on that basis would they get on board with such platforms.

So, it is not so much technology or data that is missing today as the commercial framework and the incentives that would make the various requisite industries keen to contribute data and collaborate. To offer these things, the creation of a joint framework that helps to interoperate and understand different data, and that is ready to be tapped by all ecosystem partners, is therefore indispensable. Such a framework also needs to enable the management of access and user rights, support data ownership, and enable the tools that would handle the abstraction and normalization of data – all in the name of good and saleable consumer experiences.

In the previous chapter we analysed how CSPs could evolve their business models to become trusted, reliable gatekeepers for users and usage data and how they could use this to become the central arrangers of ecosystems for Future Homes.

But none of this is to any purpose while the data is still stuck in silos. A myriad of proprietary communication protocols do not speak to each other. In the default set-up, connected devices provide their data to applications exclusively connected to them. Consequently, newly developed applications meant to support home life cannot tap into one uniform, deep data platform sourced by all devices across the home and thereby gather usage insights that could serve as a basis from which new devices and services could be developed and plugged in. The ultimate casualty is great user experience. Quite simply, if apps and devices cannot speak to one another, they cannot be truly adaptive and responsive to users' changing needs or contexts. The entire morning scenario we described in the first section of this chapter, and much more, is rendered impossible.

Breaking down data silos for the home: A brief history

There have already been numerous attempts to break up data silos. In the open source community, organizations such as the Eclipse Foundation, with the support of players like engineering specialist Bosch and Deutsche Telekom, have, for example, tried to create an open framework around the home automation platform openHAB and the Eclipse Smart Home framework.[1] But this standard has so far failed to attract the interest necessary from a wider group of developers to achieve critical mass and, thence, success. Why? Isn't it a platform and therefore bound to succeed? Well, yes, it's a platform and although it does translate different devices' communication protocols into a common language framework, it doesn't and can't actually relay usage data exchange between devices – the one important and indispensable basis for orchestrated Future Home ecosystems and good consumer experiences.[2]

Other initiatives, like Alljoyn – supported by Qualcomm, a few more industry names, and the standardization consortium oneM2M[3] – have tried to federate standards and harmonize classes of connected objects. Again, these initiatives are unlikely to be particularly successful as web developers will not understand the federated standards and will find it hard to leverage these frameworks to use connected devices as resources for their applications.

So siloed data culture seems unlikely to disappear from the industry for now. Internet giants such as Apple, Amazon and Google all have their own proprietary frameworks in place, and at the Facebook F8 Conference in April 2019, Facebook stated 'The future is private'.

Ultimately, the emergence of the Future Home must reach a point where it makes sense to all potentially involved parties to stop holding back and indulge in a joint effort that is triggered by individual profitable margins. One can expect that slowly but surely things will move in that direction, as the joint multi-billion-dollar opportunity to act as an alliance within broad-based Future Home ecosystems is eventually recognized as too big to miss.

The potential of universal translation platforms

Beyond what we've described, there is a third path that could still yield pervasive, unhindered and omni-directional data flows in the Future Home. The World Wide Web Consortium (W3C), the global web standard initiative, has proposed a unified definition of connected objects as 'things'. It divides the capabilities of any device into three elements: properties, actions and events. With these three categories, every home device can be described and individually identified. The advantage of such an 'atomic model' is that every other communication standard or framework can be disaggregated into these basic elements and thereby a 'universal translator' can be built to unlock, harmonize, and filter data from all kinds of connected devices and services at home. In another standardization move, oneM2M has put forward a list of requirements that would help create a universal standard for the Future Home.[4]

The value proposition is also to significantly reduce the cost and risk for developing and using IoT applications by shielding developers from the fragmentation of the IoT via a means to expose digital twins for things such as local software objects, and the myriad IoT technologies and standards. This is based upon providing uniform resource identifiers (URIs) as unique identifiers for things, rich metadata, as well as semantic descriptions, eg that this is a temperature sensor that reports the temperature of a given room.

While these two initiatives combined probably have all it takes to solve the problem of disparate data standards and communication protocols, they are currently only at a nascent stage. The snag is that they are so far predominantly used in research laboratories at companies like Huawei, Siemens and some start-ups like connctd.com. Siemens is a global leader in home automation, and an active contributor to initiatives like W3C Web of Things, but these initiatives are still in an early stage to deliver the promise of the Future Home.[5]

Progress, overall, though, is still limited. W3C has attracted, at time of writing, just 261 individual members to its model. That is far from sufficient critical mass to crack the silos and unlock the data needed for the Future Home. Why is the take-up of such initiatives so slow? The main challenge is that there is a lot of information about the capabilities of individual devices not yet connected to the internet. But developers would need exposure to such information and would need to understand it in order to create apps and algorithms that leverage device data. This, though, is a huge task as it would need contributions from thousands and thousands of individual device types and manufacturers to this common standard.[6]

Another key challenge is that not enough of the right incentives exist to make today's big home data owners contribute their treasures to a common framework. If they did, Future Home developers would have open access to use connected devices as input sources for their applications – standard to the way web applications are created today.

The universal blueprint for Future Home platforms

The other key constituents that would enable this chapter's 'late for work' scenario – and so much more in the Future Home – are the platform partners. In the previous chapter we itemized the diverse partners that would be needed to form the successful Future Home ecosystem: manufacturers of new connected devices; existing industry partners that provide products and services to the household in the areas of security, appliances, health, and more; the developer community needed to create new, exciting applications; and service providers that make the whole system work and improve it.

These players will not just require data but structure. Fortunately, such a structure already exists and will, as we will see, also contribute to the facilitation of data sharing. The blueprint for convening various industries to form a Future Home platform would be as shown in Figure 8.1.

Figure 8.1 Future Home – interoperability framework and six guiding imperatives

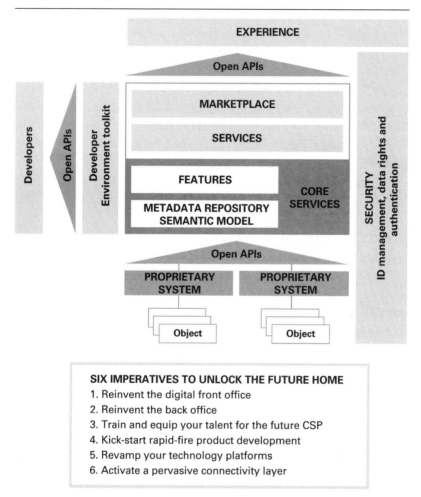

SIX IMPERATIVES TO UNLOCK THE FUTURE HOME
1. Reinvent the digital front office
2. Reinvent the back office
3. Train and equip your talent for the future CSP
4. Kick-start rapid-fire product development
5. Revamp your technology platforms
6. Activate a pervasive connectivity layer

At the core of the framework there would be a central repository for metadata and semantic modelling, ensuring interoperability across all devices and services that form a Future Home solution. Around that would be built a set of core features and services that would allow the creation of connectors to existing data sources. These would manage data acquisition and normalization, interpret and clean up data, and provide the right toolset and management levers to work with the data.

Existing Future Home ecosystems could be directly connected to these core services. Around that, there would be so-called integrated development environments (IDEs) and application programming interfaces (APIs) as standard spaces where developers could find what they needed for creating apps and services. These would include, for example, semantic search to help interpret contexts and interactions between services. Also, at the core of the framework would be the system of trust, handling security, identities, authentication, management of roles, and access and usage rights.

Service providers from various industries could add their offerings on top of this core platform, and the access to the outside world would be organized through a marketplace with open APIs as interfaces. On top of that, there would be the system of engagement and the experience layer for the end user.

In order for CSPs to be able to play a key role in this Future Home ecosystem, they themselves need to transform to become effective ecosystem orchestrators – along the six principles to unlock value that we already laid out in Chapter 6, and as illustrated in Figure 8.1.

Why the platform core should be open to everybody

All functions just described in the interoperability framework could be carried out by different business parties. The only exception should be the core services data platform, which could work along the lines of existing platforms used in finance for international and inter-institutional payment transactions. Such a platform could be collectively organized and funded by its users, while being scalable and offering partners guaranteed universal access. This is a good model because, for a Future Home platform, ownership and management by individual CSPs or other ecosystem partners would not provide sufficient neutrality. Instead, different set-ups could be used, such as putting the platform under the aegis of an industry consortium, an open source foundation or an independent organization such as W3C or the global industry association TM Forum.

The point is, it needs not only to be neutral but to have the right incentives to grow the platform's reach, to expand the number of participating parties, and to increase the appeal for the developer community. While most of these neutral institutions today focus on standard setting or creating frameworks for alignment on best practices, they would need to turn into real operators of the core platform, running software for the entire ecosystem.

Such a platform needs to manage the interests of the contributing hardware manufacturers and other industry partners so that they see value in contributing their previously siloed data buckets. There therefore needs to be a charter for data use in the Future Home that secures the interests of all data-contributing parties. Such a charter would work as the common rulebook, providing a definition of data ownership, a standard of verification for data usage and persistence of data, a standard for the management of privacy and security, a framework to manage roles, access and usage rights, and, crucially, a framework for the joint monetization of data, hardware, and services.

Build it and they will come

From a purely technological vantage point, the core platform can be built from standard components that already exist. Every home device that consumers use today – screens, ambient devices, voice-enabled devices, and many more in the future – would be capable of delivering the experience layer. Likewise, the open API management tools, components for business process orchestration, authentication flows, policy and security management can be built on standard technologies.

Some technologies within this platform architecture though will not remain static, but, by definition, will be very alive and mutable. Rules engines, for example, or AI-, cognitive- and machine-learning algorithms are constantly evolving, as are other features like lifecycle management, monetization and billing solutions, or analytic modelling support tools. Another element that will evolve is the core semantic data platform, which will be obliged to grow since it will have to understand more and more inputs as they are contributed to the 'universal translator' over time.

A joint effort will be required to attract the developer community and get them to use what is offered for crystalizing new apps and services. CSPs should therefore proactively invest in creating incentives for the ecosystem partners to start collaborating, as well as kick-starting the creation of start-ups and ventures around the Future Home.

How CSPs can lead the way to the Future Home

The Future Home will work, as we have said, because it will be built on trust, security, ethics and reliability. It will create an exceptional user experience every day, and this will reinforce the sense of it as a trusted daily companion.

CSPs will lead the way, provided they solve the tricky equation of marrying their traditional role with that of a modern platform business. They need to transform their own tech stack, turning their traditional customer relationship management-focused information technologies into a strictly user-centric IT architecture, by decoupling the network, realizing the concept of a pervasive network, and adopting new ways of working as well as building new skills and capabilities.

Finally, the different CSPs entering this market, while retaining their existing customers, will need to collaborate on a global data framework for the Future Home. Such a framework must be one in which developers feel able to access and scale the interoperability of the Future Home's devices and services. If CSPs fall short of that, they will also fail to attract enough creative power to interest users – and keep them interested – in the Future Home.

Takeaways

1 Data siloing means home life in context cannot be fully understood, as learning, adapting, and anticipating systems are ruled out – and with those, good user experience.

2 The creation of a joint data reservoir ready to be tapped by all ecosystem partners is indispensable for personalized and appealing home services.

3 The central interoperability platform that can overcome today's data silence between Future Home devices should be the responsibility of an industry-wide body and not one commercial player.

9

The road to the Future Home

CHAPTER SUMMARY

....

In this book we have mapped a paradigm-shifting terrain, one in which the Future Home will learn, adapt to and anticipate our needs. It will no longer be defined by the walls, floors and roof. Instead the Future Home will make you feel at home, anywhere. This promises us a vast array of new opportunities and experiences. We have provided glimpses of how some of them will look in practice and itemized the suite of new technologies, with 5G at the centre, that will make this possible. We have discussed the new structures businesses will have to adopt to capitalize on this enormous opportunity, and identified communications service providers (CSPs) as best placed to run the platforms supporting devices and services for the Future Home. In this final chapter, we reflect on this journey, summarizing it to create an easily referenced guide for businesses entering the Future Home market, and looking forward to the exciting, and very profitable, futures they can expect.

....

As should now be clear, the digitally enabled Future Home 5G is a great deal more than just the next step from today's connected homes. It is born of sophisticated ecosystems, offering residents high-quality day-to-day services and in that regard it amounts to a massive new business and growth opportunity for a broad range of hardware products, platforms and services.

The new world is already taking shape. Where current connected homes are supported by a limited number of devices, most of which hardly communicate with one another, the Future Home will contain hundreds if not thousands of devices, apps, and services, virtually all able to share data and collaborate, with the common goal of outstanding consumer experience. This seamless environment will be able to follow the inhabitants even when they leave the physical space of home, anticipating their needs and facilitating their routines everywhere.

The 5G wireless standard will be the great enabler of this new actively mindful home environment, complemented by a suite of other new technologies. The embedded SIM format will make sure that even the smallest devices can communicate data. Edge computing will allow for ultra-low latency data processing. Semantic interoperability will enable connected things and services to interact with each other and make it easy for web developers to solve real consumer problems. And machine learning, AI, and advanced data analytics will allow for the advanced pre-emptive 'thinking' and acting of the Future Home.

But at the heart of it all will be the needs of the consumer. To pay good money for it, the potential Future Home resident must see it as something that enhances his or her life specifically, not just an off-the-shelf, one-size-fits-all solution. This user-centredness must be the strict guideline for any business participating in Future Home ecosystems. The concept can only take off when lasting quality is offered and consumer trust maintained throughout.

Life closely intertwined with technology

At the beginning of the book we saw an example of how this would work as early as 2030, following a single man through a day in his life with the Future Home in the 5G era. From the moment he awoke, through his meals, commute, workday, and leisure time, he was assisted by connected, sometimes roboticized or automated, versions of numerous ordinary household objects, including windows, curtains, vacuum, thermostats, the coffee maker, and more.

We saw how these devices were able to collaborate, and how the home itself was able to adapt to changing circumstances. It suggested an alternative mode of transport to work when the usual means became unavailable – and then subtly adjusted the man's diet to account for the extra effort involved. And we saw how home transcended physical boundaries, making even a hot-desk situation feel personal and familiar, then later enabling, via virtual reality, an intense emotional bonding session with the man's mother, though she was geographically far away.

The socio-demographic megatrends shaping hyper-connected lifestyles

Building on this, we looked at the socio-demographic factors taking us towards the Future Home. Megatrends shaping hyper-connected lifestyles were identified. These include the way daily life is already becoming more and more personalized and connected by technology, and the way the younger generations, Millennials and Generation Z, who've grown up surrounded by this technology, will shape development of the Future Home.

These generations' predilections will mean, in particular, that Future Homes are oriented much more towards Do It For Me (DIFM) than Do It Yourself (DIY). Consumers will want easy technology set-ups into which new devices and apps can plug and play in seconds. At the same time, another profound influence but from the opposite direction will be that of the majority ageing population, creating huge demand for services such as digital home healthcare.

In the same light, we identified key consumer mindsets, defined as combinations of 'Showstoppers', 'Nestlers', 'Navigators' and 'Explorers', with further definition provided by 'with children' and 'without'. Businesses must study such mindsets closely and further come to understand individual

Future Home customers via their behaviour. They must not try to lead consumers with technology, but instead provide tech stacks for individual lifestyles, and then be ready to adapt repeatedly as new needs and predilections arise.

The great variety of specific use cases

Based on these categorizations, we went on to look at an example of family life, showing how the Future Home, with easy plug-and-play tech, can intelligently assist with childcare, get to know and respond to each family member individually, and foster togetherness.

We then looked at an example of 'ageing in place' – a senior with depleted function being able to remain at home rather than moving to a care facility. This showed how an ordinary home could become a Future Home, with the introduction of a multitude of intelligent, interoperable and intercommunicating technologies to provide the specific care required. It also showed how one Future Home will often need to communicate with another, with the senior in question monitored remotely from the home of family members living far away.

Fragmentation: The barrier to development of the Future Home

To allow businesses to chart their journey towards the sophisticated Future Home scenarios we have been describing, we examined the question of what has held up progress so far. In a nutshell, attempts at connected homes have, up to now, been marred by fragmentation: a mix of different hardware and software standards, point-to-point architectures, protocols, and radio standards, as well as heavy data siloing.

We studied the various business players that will be key to the Future Home – communications service providers (CSPs), device and hardware manufacturers, platform and app providers, and traditional service companies – and how all have so far failed to overcome the critical hurdles, largely because they have acted independently rather than forging the critical conflict-free partnerships within powerful ecosystem platforms.

Their intransigence or mere lack of awareness of the need for change and collaboration has created the widespread data silence at home. Hence devices and services, up to now, have been unable to communicate and share data freely, making it impossible to provide the kind of seamless user experience and hyper-connected domestic life we described in our opening scenario.

5G: The connectivity game changer

What difference will 5G, the newest generation of cellular technology, make? Well, it's a quantum leap from its predecessor, offering much greater speeds, lower latency, more security and, crucially, the ability to handle 10 times more devices at any one time – around one million devices per square kilometre – vital in the device-rich Future Home. These advantages alone make clear what a massive business opportunity this breakthrough technology represents.

It meets consumer demands for easy plug and play because, unlike with Wi-Fi and other protocols, devices can connect to it automatically – just as your phone connects to your cellular network today. That will finally establish interoperability and override the organically grown mish-mash of inconsistent devices, data and connectivity standards in today's connected homes – opening the door to an endless spectrum of possible paid-for, high-quality home services.

The need to build consumer trust via the strongest possible security, privacy and ethics

But for businesses eyeing the burgeoning Future Home market, the challenges only begin here. A paradox of the Future Home is that data must flow freely between a multitude of actors but must also be kept secure and private. Relatedly, the Future Home's AI must be able to learn our behaviour but not use the information inappropriately or act against us.

We argue that Future Home ecosystem orchestrators must therefore ensure that the data flowing so freely across their area of responsibility is also sealed securely within it and not misused by human or machine. We also argue that CSPs, due to their long-term status as deeply trusted providers of watertight security for home connectivity set-ups, are businesses that are strong contenders to be these orchestrators: platform administrators for the Future Home.

Future Home orchestrators and gatekeepers: CSPs reloaded

In addition to the long-term consumer trust we have just described, two further factors also put CSPs in pole position to be the Future Home's platform orchestrators: experience of keeping good customer relationships, and the ability to deliver mission-critical infrastructure. The change to the business set-up and value chain this will require will be a root-and-branch transformation altering the very structure and culture of these businesses from hierarchical to horizontal, from linear to agile.

It will entail revamping the business's technology platform, and both the front and back office, effectively embedding software tools with the same levels of sophistication as those that will define the Future Home. Staff must be trained in the radically new skills they will need to operate effectively in this new world. Rapid-fire product development must be kick-started in order to keep pace with the ever-changing demands of Future Home users. And, of course, all of this will need to be bound together using a new pervasive connectivity layer, powered by – what else? – 5G.

A necessary shift in business model

This drastic change requires a considerable shift in strategy away from legacy business models towards new business lines while core incumbent operations are kept going profitably on a digitally streamlined basis.

First, the existing core business must be repositioned with the help of digital technology, the main aim being to reduce cost and free up investment capacity. This allows the organization as a whole to venture into novel business lines such as the emerging services market around the Future Home.

Second, the push into such new business opportunities should be conducted with caution. The core of the organization cannot afford a slip; it must keep growing to steady the ship – more so, as it often takes longer than initially thought until new business models yield positive economic results.

Third, venturing into the new Future Home market will involve a paradigm shift from 'first time right' to 'fail fast and learn'. It will involve a little trial and error, to test and iterate. Finding the right role and profitable set-up in a protracted structure such as a Future Home ecosystem is not done overnight. But once a specific approach shows initial profitable results it should be scaled quickly. Future Home services are end-user services. Some of them could go in and out of fashion with consumers at a regular pace. So it is advisable to make the most of them while they last. The overall rule should therefore be to identify the right entry points in the Future Home market and then scale quickly.

On this journey, CSPs will begin to operate multi-sided platforms and play a pivotal orchestrator role at the centre of Future Home ecosystems, rather than being just integrators of monolithic infrastructure like in their old days. Hence they will be shifting investments from physical network to software, basing their innovation paradigm on a partner ecosystem and changing the skills and capabilities of their workforce, not only in IT and technology, but even more so in their traditional sales, service and marketing departments.

Attracting partners to attract consumers

Such is the situation for the Future Home platform orchestrators. What about the other stakeholders, the ecosystem partners who will provide the devices and services without which it will be impossible to attract consumers? As should be clear by now, the opportunities for providing services to the Future Home are vast and varied, ranging across disciplines and sectors including energy management, health, entertainment, e-commerce, finance, healthcare, fitness, education, communications, and much more. Also vital will be more technical specialists in areas such as edge computing and AI.

It should also be clear from the sheer number of requirements that CSPs will not be able to continue their old model of simply creating and marketing their own services as add-ons to their communications and connectivity offerings. This is another reason why it makes sense for them to become platforms, orchestrating the increasingly vast ecosystem of specialized providers. Here, the pathbeaters are the providers of digital voice assistants such as Amazon's Alexa.

In order to manage all of this, the platform will need to be designed to harvest data from all the control points in the ecosystem – devices and services such as telephony, the cloud, payment and messaging services, and much more. Such data harvesting will be vital to the creation of the incredibly tailored and intelligent user experiences we have looked at in this book. But it can also only be justified to users if that experience is consistently excellent.

Breaking down data silos to benefit both users and ecosystem players

It will be a considerable challenge just to attract and orchestrate all the necessary ecosystem partners. Key to this will be getting them to break out of the persistent data siloing that prevents them from creating devices and services that can communicate freely. Without this free sharing of information, of course, the Future Home is an impossibility as the ecosystem as a whole will be unable to learn, adapt to, and anticipate user needs.

Bear in mind, also, that a free flow of information will not just be necessary within individual Future Homes, but between two or more. And the Future Home will also need to be able to communicate with the numerous services outside it that occupants will want to access – especially if they are to feel at home everywhere.

The solution must be the creation of a joint data reservoir that can be tapped by all relevant organizations. To overcome participants' hesitancy on data sharing, we finished by recommending the creation of a central interoperability platform run by a neutral industry-wide body.

CSPs at the crossroads

The Future Home is an opportunity like few others. The task of transitioning to it is clearly enormous, but CSPs that opt not to plunge ahead as platform orchestrators should be under no illusion: if they do not lead, they will have to follow. This paradigm shift is happening with or without them. The seeming security of their vertical integration models is not a place they will be able to stay even if they want to.

But the Future Home is not just a mountain that cannot be avoided. It is also an opportunity too good to miss. By providing seamless technology such as 5G, by removing interoperability hurdles and by becoming the trusted partners of consumers, CSPs will unlock the potential for growth and innovation for all participants in the Future Home ecosystem. Accenture Strategy research on the relationship between trust and financial performance shows that in the telecommunications industry, a *material* increase in trust relates to a 0.3 per cent increase in revenue growth and a 1.0 per cent increase in EBITDA growth.[1]

Building on this trust, CSPs can act as guide, consultant and partner during the 5G-driven digital transformation journey of their customers. By co-creating carrier-grade, turn-key solutions and additional services successfully, they create even more trust in their customer relationships.

CSPs with the courage and vision to transition from their old business models to the new Future Home platform orchestrator position will increase their opportunities to monetize services to an absolutely enormous extent. Benefiting from network effects, they will profit from apps and services without even having to take a hand in their development. And they will become the managers of almost incalculable quantities of the most valuable asset of our time: data.

TAKEAWAYS AT A GLANCE

Chapter 2: Consumer needs in a hyper-connected world

1 Megatrends such as the emergence of hyper-connected lifestyles, the tech savviness of younger generations, ageing in place and a 'do it for me' attitude will define variations of the Future Home market.

2 The specific mindsets of all sorts of Future Home user types can be pinpointed as a distinct mix between 'Showstoppers', 'Nestlers', 'Explorers' and 'Navigators'.

3 Businesses catering to the Future Home market should take sociodemographic types as the starting point for technological solutions – not the other way around.

Chapter 3: From use cases to business cases

1 Modern life is busy and therefore people are keen to automate mundane tasks, resolve current issues and predict future risks. To match these demands, home technology must be tailored to residents' real needs in order to be effective.

2 Convenience and hassle-free plug-and-play functionality creates optimal user experience.

3 Thoughtfully applied, tech can bond people at home rather than rendering them 'alone together'.

4 Future Home use cases can also relieve the pressure on society: ageing in place in the Future Home, for example.

Chapter 4: Turning homes into 5G Future Homes

1 Today's connected homes harbour a plethora of incoherent device, protocol and radio standards that can be consolidated in one go by 5G.

2 5G and its segmented spectrum is ideally suited to create and enable new applications in the Future Home as it can fluidly balance speed, low latency and number of devices connected.

3 But 5G needs complementary technologies such as eSIM, edge computing and AI to reach its full experience potential.

Chapter 5: Privacy and security: Two separate challenges of the 5G Future Home

1 At today's technology levels, a bad actor wanting to gain access to current connected homes has a high chance of success.

2 The Future Home industry and users need to have a clear position on standards for securing the storage and management of personal data, with users having first-hand control.

3 CSPs have a strong hand to play, with an advantage being incumbent consumer trust and a hitherto very high data privacy and data security record.

Chapter 6: The rise of the connected living ecosystem builder

1 CSP businesses enjoy a head start in the race for the Future Home as they combine high consumer trust with close customer relationships and gate-keeping connectivity infrastructure.

2   But the CSP sector needs to revamp its approach, digitize its front and back offices, train talent for the new service world and adopt quicker product development cycles.

3   It is paramount for CSPs to build agile platform businesses that can accommodate ecosystems involving a wide array of partners.

Chapter 7: Emerging business models for the Future Home

1   The multi-sided platform is at the heart of the success of Amazon, and the hitherto vertically siloed CSPs need to grasp the benefits of such platforms.

2   Opening up, controlling and managing data, instead of infrastructure, will allow CSPs to create advanced Future Home data management services that hold higher margin value for themselves and trusted partners.

3   Any CSP remaining in its 'walled garden' should be under no illusion: it will have to change anyway, one way or another. CSPs need to become open ecosystem orchestrators building on relevance, scalability, experience and trust.

Chapter 8: Creating incentives for the Future Home ecosystem

1   Data siloing means home life in context cannot be fully understood, as learning, adapting, and anticipating systems are ruled out – and with those, good user experience.

2   The creation of a joint data reservoir ready to be tapped by all ecosystem partners is indispensable for personalized and appealing home services.

3   The central interoperability platform that can overcome today's data silence between Future Home devices should be the responsibility of an industry-wide body and not one commercial player.

GLOSSARY OF TERMS

4G LTE standard: The radio standard currently used in mobile communication, following on from previous standards such as 2G and 3G. The acronym stands for 'fourth generation long-term evolution'. Its introduction in 2009, initially in Scandinavian countries, increased data speeds by five to seven times compared to its predecessor. Nevertheless, 4G's download speeds are considered too slow to form the basis for the high-quality service experiences Future Home users would demand.

5G wireless standard: A term colloquially used for the latest internationally agreed wireless radio standard. 5G stands for 'fifth generation' – representing the fifth upgrade since the universal GSM mobile standard was introduced more than 25 years ago. Already in use in some countries, 5G is expected to roll out across all major industrialized regions during 2020. It has clear advantages over older standards: it is 10 times as fast as its predecessor standard 4G LTE, reducing latency to milliseconds. Its data capacity is also significantly higher, while 5G is also the first such standard where objects are directly connected and managed by the network. These features make 5G the ideal standard for applications in the Future Home.

Advanced analytics: A set of data analytics tools sophisticated enough to find hidden patterns and predict behaviour and trends from usage data or other data sets. The ability to mine and clean data for use by advanced analytics tools is essential for the techniques to be successful. Really a suite of capabilities, advanced analytics includes machine learning, semantic analysis, pattern matching and various statistical and simulation methods, among others.

Ageing in place: Health and home care applications will form a huge chunk of the emerging string of services around the Future Home. The concept of ageing in place foresees elderly individuals living independently for much longer in the homes they have inhabited, often for decades. Intelligent digital technology can do a lot to make ageing in place a widespread and affordable reality. Various devices fitted with sensors and cameras can help to supervise an elderly person's well-being even from far away – giving senior citizens a good standard of living even into very old age.

'Alone together': A phenomenon observable in the digital era that affects groups of friends or family members. Individuals, even when physically present with each other, become overly absorbed by digital devices, resulting in loneliness due to the lack of human interaction such as conversations or joint walks. Any Future Home set-up must take this drawback into account and make sure the home interrupts people in their digital activities when 'alone together' sets in.

Artificial intelligence (AI): A software concept dating back to the 1950s that is only now taking off as data collection and processing capacity become both sufficiently powerful and affordable. AI encompasses algorithms that can use large data sets to learn, recognize, remember and take decisions. The principal input of such learning processes is vast amounts of suitable data from which the system can draw its conclusions and act. Where AI works in close proximity to humans, such as in the Future Home, it must be secured so that humans can always override its decisions at any given moment.

'At home anywhere': Where first-generation connected homes were little more than walls and a roof containing some rudimentary digital home technology, the concept of the Future Home expands the notion of home to 'at home anywhere'. In such a scenario, a home, serving as a support hub for hyper-connected lifestyles and enabled by artificial intelligence (AI), advanced data analytics and other technologies, expands its services into locations far away, into hotel or meeting rooms, holiday resorts, co-working spaces or even old neighbourhoods.

Back office: Within the context of a CSP, this term comprises a central function running the network, backing up the services offered to end customers. In the traditional set-up of a telecommunications provider, this has been a strongly siloed unit. Within the emerging operating model of pervasive networks, typical for the sector, a CSP's back office must adopt agile principles and become responsive to end customer demands and instant service trends forming in the consumer markets.

Bluetooth: A short-wave wireless radio communication standard for network connections at small distances. The primary goal of its developers was to replace cables between consumer electronics devices such as, for example, a laptop and a headset. In connected home or even Future Home environments Bluetooth is disadvantaged as a network technology to connect home tech devices due to its short data communication range.

Cloud computing: A data-handling architecture sending data into the 'cloud' to centralized and remote server farms and data warehouses for further processing, analysis and storage, rather than keeping the data close to where it has been created, on local servers or on PC hard drives. Cloud computing has its advantages, as professional cloud services offer proper data backup, security management, data cleaning and analytics tools. But the technology also has limits when it comes to the Future Home, where residents will expect ultra-low-latent, experience-rich services and the time delays often associated with cloud solutions stand in the way of a good user experience.

Connected home tech stacks: The connected home of today is made up of tech stacks comprising components with almost no data communication between them, because device types, data formats and protocols are far from standardized across the industry. Home tech devices are also often designed to serve only one single service purpose, with no involvement from other devices. Devices such as intelligent thermostats, smart doorbells and lighting systems currently work as insular proprietary solutions with no interface to any other technology in the home. In the Future Home, in order to genuinely anticipate and meet user needs intelligently, devices will need to share data and collaborate.

CSP: An industry acronym standing for 'communications service provider', CSPs are a group of businesses comprising traditional telecommunications operators active in fixed-line and mobile telephony, as well as cable and satellite network operators and providers of managed services. This book sees CSPs as ideal contenders to capture the gatekeeper and orchestrator role within emerging Future Home ecosystems.

DIFM: The four letters refer to 'Do it For Me', a mentality contrasted with DIY, describing a consumer who demands tailored home tech solutions that work 'out of the box' with no additional set-up configuration or complicated cabling. The DIFM mentality is mainly associated with younger generations who were born into the digital era. This age group is used to self-starting technology occupying minimal user headspace. The Future Home market can only prosper once tech vendors take this mentality on board and design their products, services and customer interaction accordingly.

Digital omni-channel platform (DOCP): A digital platform concept designed by Accenture to offer end customers of CSPs a seamless experience across all possible channels of interaction, be it online, in store, at call centres, via mobile apps, or through social media. The DOCP uses advanced data analytics, cognitive computing and AI as well as process automation to make interaction and communication with a CSP customer as precise and relevant as possible – forming the basis for both much better user experience and lower operational cost.

DIY: Or 'Do it yourself'. In the context of this book, this describes the current, relatively substandard version of a digitized home, one in which the resident must perform detailed and awkward set-up processes to get home technology going.

Ecosystem: In the context of this book, ecosystems are individually tailored alliances and partnerships from a wide spectrum of companies – ranging from CSPs to device manufacturers to app developers – with the aim of delivering a specific Future Home service. Each participant in such networks benefits from the combinatorial augmentation of their input, resulting not only in profitable new business lines for ecosystem partners but also in unprecedented service levels for the consumer.

Edge computing: A novel approach to decentralize data processing capacity by positioning a processor unit such as a server right on the 'edge' of a network – avoiding long-distance data flows to centralized cloud servers in a faraway data warehouse. This has a key advantage in the context of the Future Home: speed. Home tech devices, often with their own edge computing units on board, can communicate at short distance at lightning speed, thus delivering instant service at practically no latency – which makes the concept the ideal complement to the already low-latency 5G network.

eSIM: A firmly installed SIM card in mobile devices such as smartphones or home tech items such as thermostats, lights or smart blinds. SIMs (subscriber identity modules) are necessary to connect any device to a wireless network such as 5G. eSIMS have the crucial advantages of being programmable and able to adapt to any network the device wants to connect to without the need for a new physical SIM card. That gives home device manufacturers the freedom not to have to build devices for specific networks – the eSIMS are just reprogrammed. From a user point of view the devices can be programmed to pick the most affordable network offered.

Front office: Traditionally, the part of a CSP organization dealing with end customers. Like the back office, the front office for the Future Home must become much more receptive to instant customer demands and market trends, relying on pervasive networks with perpetual data exchange, including data sharing with the back office.

Future Home tech stacks: An advanced set of technologies securing a maximum of consumer experience at home. 5G and complementary technologies such as eSIM, edge computing and AI can be collectively configured to deliver best-quality user experience and life enhancement in a Future Home.

Gen Z: People born after 1995 but before 2015. Gen Z is the youngest and most tech-savvy consumer group so far, having grown up not only with the internet, but also the experience of ubiquitous connectivity, meaning they take all this for granted. It's a mindset everybody who is seeking a share of the emerging Future Home market must cater to. Gen Z also has a DIFM attitude, expecting tech-based service providers to deliver easy-to-handle plug-and-play devices with minimal user input required for installation.

Hyper-connected lifestyle: Our era deserves the epithet 'hyper-connected', with petabytes of data and information circling around the globe each day. Not so long ago, people sent faxes, placed land-line phone calls or sent letters. By these basic standards today's world looks vastly advanced with its ubiquitous internet-based communication hardware and software run on wireless and fixed-line networks.

Hyper-personalization: Catering for a unique customer with a tailored offering has always been seen as an attractive point of differentiation by providers of products and services. But only with the wholesale digital transformation of consumer life has the promise of mass-personalized services or products become a compelling reality. Once users allow their usage data to be shared with service or product designers and even third parties, the era of hyper-personalization can begin. Product makers can now see in real time how consumers use a device, what tailored service could be offered on the back of it, and how the product must be redesigned to match the needs of individual customers.

Internet of Things (IoT): Also referred to as the Internet of Everything, the term captures the evolving internet-connected world in which exponentially increasing numbers of objects can data communicate via the net. It is expected that almost every hardware item in the world will at some point become connected. Widespread data links between objects form the basis for advanced services. Hardware items can then offer these to their users.

Last mile: A piece of legacy communication infrastructure, copper wire or fibre-optic cable, connecting a home to the wider network running in the street. This bit of wiring is crucial for the delivery of advanced services to the individual home. From the first emergence of broadband internet, the 'last mile' was a bottleneck to speed and data capacity. With 5G a complete replacement of such fixed wiring could happen through fast wireless networks – opening up massive opportunities for advanced Future Home services.

Millennials: Also dubbed Gen Y, Millennials form the age group preceding Gen Z, and are another subset of 'digital natives', key tech-savvy consumer groups to be kept in mind by all industries targeting Future Home markets. As a statistical cohort, it roughly comprises people born between 1980 and 1995, meaning they witnessed the birth and fast spread of the mass-consumer internet. This primed them to be susceptible to connected lifestyles if not yet the hyper-connected ones Gen Z expects.

Multi-sided platform effects: Digital platforms, if set up shrewdly in a specific market, produce economic effects beneficial to all sides. On the one side, a platform's organizers benefit from data insights gathered through the platform. On the other, end users enjoy the data-induced improvement, precision and personalization of the services delivered by the platform. These mutual benefits for all make platform businesses grow exponentially compared to conventional businesses. Good examples for the study of these effects are Amazon's online shopping or Uber's transportation platforms.

Navigators and Explorers: Two home user mindsets, micro-profiled as personas by Accenture, that reflect extremes in consumer attitudes towards tech. While Explorers are early-adopting types keen to try out the latest products and services, at the other end of the spectrum the Navigators need to find real value or necessity in a product before going all in. Both personas must be considered when Future Home services or devices are designed.

New tech enablers: The Future Home can only become reality due to a raft of breakthrough technologies that recently have become available for mass deployment. Next to the 5G wireless standard there are three main complementary technologies helping 5G to live up to its great enabler role in the Future Home: eSIMs, artificial intelligence and edge computing – all three allowing compact, intelligence-driven devices to respond with ultra-low latency.

Pervasive network: A novel type of data network architecture run by a CSP where – in the experience of the user – connectivity is unobtrusive yet always available. Pervasive computing forms the basis of pervasive networks, a concept that combines existing network technologies with wireless computing, voice recognition, internet capability and AI. Advanced technologies such as 5G, software-defined networking (SDN), network function virtualization (NFV), AI, robotic process automation (RPA) and blockchain are emerging as enabler components of the pervasive network approach, with the potential to combine in unpredictable new ways. For outstanding consumer experience, a pervasive network would be the ideal basis from which to cater for the Future Home market.

Showstoppers and Nestlers: Two home user mindsets, micro-profiled as personas by Accenture, that define extremes of personality applicable for the Future Home market. While the more outgoing Showstopper type sees the home as an opportunity to reflect their personal 'brand', the more discreet and inward-looking Nestler type values privacy and comfort at home. Both personas need consideration when Future Home services or devices are designed.

URI: Uniform resource identifier. It is a set of characters identifying names or resources on the Internet. Such identifiers describe, for instance, which computer carries which resource and how these resources can be accessed.

User experience: A compelling user experience will be a make-or-break criterion when it comes to developing the Future Home market. This experience must amount to a performance of home tech that gives residents the feeling that their home is a companion or assistant throughout daily life, one that can anticipate and respond to needs – regardless of a resident's location. 5G technology will be crucial to achieve these advanced user experience levels.

Vertical business model: A business model with the ambition to cover vast stretches of the production and distribution process of a hardware product or a service. Applied to CSPs, verticality means that these businesses see themselves as providers of connectivity infrastructure to homes, complemented by a few extra services around this core product. To become a key player in the Future Home market, CSPs should give up on their verticality and set up less hierarchical multi-sided platform models where they take the role of the trusted platform orchestrator, data custodian and service gatekeeper to the home.

Voice-controlled devices: Hardware items that can, due to advanced speech recognition software, detect and understand languages semantically and respond to human voice questions. A range of assistant speakers already use advanced speech recognition, though the technology is also promising as a user interface in the context of Future Home services.

Wi-Fi: A wireless network technology that provides fast internet connections in public or private environments. In conventional connected homes, the Wi-Fi radio standard typically connects devices such as laptops, smartphones or tablets with a router providing the fixed-line gateway to the internet. Beyond that, other home hardware such as doorbells, thermostats, smart meters or domestic appliances, are more and more connected via Wi-Fi. The standard is unsuitable for advanced Future Home applications as its bandwidth capacity is limited and its range is only around 20 to 30 metres in buildings.

Wireless spectrum: A defined range of electromagnetic waves made available by regulators for commercial use. The wireless spectrum is divided up into different bands, sub-divided into frequencies used by different networks.

Z-Wave: A wireless radio communication standard used in connected home networks to connect devices such as thermostats, doorbells and window sensors. It was developed as a simpler, even more affordable alternative to Zigbee, and is more power-efficient compared to Wi-Fi.

Zigbee: An open wireless standard that has been developed to serve as a data network between devices. Running Zigbee networks in a connected home is relatively low cost and, compared to Wi-Fi, the devices consume only small amounts of power once they are connected to the standard.

ENDNOTES

Acknowledgements

1 https://www.accenture.com/us-en/insights/living-business/future-home (archived at https://perma.cc/PQ7L-XER4)

Chapter 2

1 IDC (2019) The growth in connected IoT devices is expected to generate 79.4ZB of data in 2025, According to a New IDC forecast [online] https://www.idc.com/getdoc.jsp?containerId=prUS45213219 (archived at https://perma.cc/RNG6-HVJV)

2 Kosciulek, A, Varricchio, T and Stickles, N (2019) Millennials are willing to spend $5000 or more on vacation, making them the age group that spends the most on travel — but Gen Z isn't far behind, *Business Insider* [online] https://www.businessinsider.com/millennials-spend-5000-on-vacation-age-group-spends-the-most-on-travel-but-gen-z-isnt-far-behind-2019-4 (archived at https://perma.cc/ERW6-GJ4M)

3 Searing, L (2019) The big number: Millennials to overtake Boomers in 2019 as the largest US population group, *Washington Post* [online] https://www.washingtonpost.com/national/health-science/the-big-number-millennials-to-overtake-boomers-in-2019-as-largest-us-population-group/2019/01/25/a566e636-1f4f-11e9-8e21-59a09ff1e2a1_story.html?utm_term=.2a3e1457f5e4 (archived at https://perma.cc/576G-9RJZ)

4 Tilford, C (2018) The millennial moment – in charts, *Financial Times* [online] https://www.ft.com/content/f81ac17a-68ae-11e8-b6eb-4acfcfb08c11 (archived at https://perma.cc/3QX2-YDQE)

5 United Nations (2018) The world's cities in 2018 [online] https://www.un.org/en/events/citiesday/assets/pdf/the_worlds_cities_in_2018_data_booklet.pdf (archived at https://perma.cc/Y7BJ-2N6W)

6 Ibid

7 Fry, R (2018) Millennials are the largest generation in the U.S. labor force, *Pew Research Center* [online] https://www.pewresearch.org/fact-tank/2018/04/11/millennials-largest-generation-us-labor-force/ (archived at https://perma.cc/7JZD-JYP5)

8 Tilford, C (2018) The millennial moment: in charts, *Financial Times* [online] https://www.ft.com/content/f81ac17a-68ae-11e8-b6eb-4acfcfb08c11 (archived at https://perma.cc/3QX2-YDQE)

9 Ibid

10 Fuscaldo, D (2018) Home buying goes high-tech as millennials become largest real estate buyers, *Forbes* [online] https://www.forbes.com/sites/donnafuscaldo/2018/09/26/home-buying-goes-high-tech-as-millennials-become-largest-real-estate-buyers/#11a90e3b7774 (archived at https://perma.cc/BU27-2HWN)

11 Accenture (nd) The race to the smart home: Why Communications Service Providers must defend and grow this critical market [online] https://www.accenture.com/_acnmedia/pdf-50/accenture-race-to-the-smart-home.pdf (archived at https://perma.cc/KKZ6-W7M5)

12 Ibid

13 Accenture (nd) The race to the smart home [online] https://www.accenture.com/t20180529T062408Z__w__/us-en/_acnmedia/PDF-50/Accenture-Race-To-The-Smart-Home.pdf (archived at https://perma.cc/9WGH-UUHW)

14 Accenture (2019) Millennial and Gen Z consumers paving the way for non-traditional care models, Accenture study finds [online] https://newsroom.accenture.com/news/millennial-and-gen-z-consumers-paving-the-way-for-non-traditional-care-models-accenture-study-finds.htm (archived at https://perma.cc/DA67-EZGY)

15 Ibid

16 The Council of Economic Advisers (2014) 15 economic facts about Millennials [online] https://obamawhitehouse.archives.gov/sites/default/files/docs/millennials_report.pdf (archived at https://perma.cc/D5TK-PMAM) page 9, figure 4

17 Donnelly, C and Scaff, R (nd) Who are the millennial shoppers? And what do they really want? *Accenture* [online] https://www.accenture.com/us-en/insight-outlook-who-are-millennial-shoppers-what-do-they-really-want-retail (archived at https://perma.cc/C4X6-QKX3)

18 United Nations (2019) World population prospects 2019 [online] https://population.un.org/wpp2019/DataQuery/ (archived at https://perma.cc/3RX7-B22G)

19 AARP (2018) Stats and facts from the 2018 AARP Home and Community Preferences Survey [online] https://www.aarp.org/livable-communities/about/info-2018/2018-aarp-home-and-community-preferences-survey.html (archived at https://perma.cc/97WA-5FRM)

20 Accenture, based on United Nations World Population Prospects 2019 [online] https://population.un.org/wpp/ (archived at https://perma.cc/95VL-U6LW)

21 University of British Columbia (2017) Using money to buy time linked to increased happiness, *Eureka Alert* [online] https://www.eurekalert.org/pub_releases/2017-07/uobc-umt072017.php (archived at https://perma.cc/QX66-938C)

22 Accenture (nd) Putting the human first in the Future Home [online] https://www.accenture.com/_acnmedia/pdf-98/accenture-putting-human-first-future-home.pdf (archived at https://perma.cc/7ZJD-Q677)

23 Ibid; https://in.accenture.com/thedock/futurehome/ (archived at https://perma.cc/5VBH-KVGQ)

24 Ibid

25 Ibid

Chapter 4

1 Accenture (nd) The race to the smart home: Why communications service providers must defend and grow this critical market [online] https://www.accenture.com/_acnmedia/PDF-50/Accenture-Race-To-The-Smart-Home.pdf#zoom=50 (archived at https://perma.cc/NLD2-YGSD)

2 Oreskovic, A (2014) Google to acquire Nest for $3.2 billion in cash, *Reuters* [online] https://www.reuters.com/article/us-google-nest/google-to-acquire-nest-for-3-2-billion-in-cash-idUSBREA0C1HP20140113 (archived at https://perma.cc/5GGK-CLLF); Team, T (2014) Google's strategy behind The $3.2 billion acquisition of Nest Labs, *Forbes* [online] https://www.forbes.com/sites/greatspeculations/2014/01/17/googles-strategy-behind-the-3-2-billion-acquisition-of-nest-labs/#79c2d20a1d45 (archived at https://perma.cc/TG6F-G265)

3 Schaeffer, E and Sovie, D (2019) *Reinventing the Product: How to transform your business and create value in the digital age,* Kogan Page, London

4 Accenture; all prices from Home Depot, correct at time of writing

5 Business Wire (2018) The smart home is creating frustrated consumers: more than 1 in 3 US adults experience issues setting up or operating a connected device [online] https://www.businesswire.com/news/home/20180130005463/en/Smart-Home-Creating-Frustrated-Consumers-1-3 (archived at https://perma.cc/XNF7-C42T)

6 Liu, J (2019) Many smart home users still find DIY products difficult to manage, *asmag* [online] https://www.asmag.com/showpost/28346.aspx (archived at https://perma.cc/D6R5-RA7L)

7 Accenture (nd) Putting the human first in the Future Home [online] https://www.accenture.com/_acnmedia/PDF-98/Accenture-Putting-Human-First-Future-Home.pdf#zoom=50 (archived at https://perma.cc/4JVZ-ADU9)

8 Line 1: Cisco WiFi – https://www.cisco.com/c/en/us/solutions/collateral/enterprise-networks/802-11ac-solution/q-and-a-c67-734152.html (archived at https://perma.cc/K9PB-KCZY); Line 3: 3GPP Release 15 – https://www.3gpp.org/release-15 (archived at https://perma.cc/ZG87-VJCA); Line 4: 3GPP LTE Specs – https://www.3gpp.org/technologies/keywords-acronyms/97-lte-advanced (archived at https://perma.cc/G5S8-E9ZT)

9 IEEE Spectrum (nd) 3GPP Release 15 Overview: 3rd Generation Partnership Project (3GPP) members meet regularly to collaborate and create cellular communications standards [online] https://spectrum.ieee.org/telecom/wireless/3gpp-release-15-overview (archived at https://perma.cc/5KGQ-DXRL)

10 Accenture; based on Global System for Mobile Communications (GSM) and 3GPP standards:
- 1G – Advanced Mobile Phone System, Nordic Mobile Telephone, Total Access Communications System, TZ-801, TZ-802, and TZ-803
- 2G – 3GPP Phase 1
- 3G – 3GPP Release 99
- 4G – 3GPP Release 8
- 5G – 3GPP Release 15

11 Vespa, H (2018) The graying of America: more older adults than kids by 2035, *United States Census Bureau* [online] https://www.census.gov/library/stories/2018/03/graying-america.html (archived at https://perma.cc/PE28-S246)

12 Arandjelovic, R (nd) 1 million IoT devices per square Km – are we ready for the 5G transformation? *Medium* [online] https://medium.com/clx-forum/1-million-iot-devices-per-square-km-are-we-ready-for-the-5g-transformation-5d2ba416a984 (archived at https://perma.cc/9TKK-N6BD)

13 GSMA (nd) What is eSIM? [online] https://www.gsma.com/esim/about/ (archived at https://perma.cc/YRC5-8NB2)

14 GSMA (nd) eSIM [online] https://www.gsma.com/esim/ (archived at https://perma.cc/YRC5-8NB2)

Chapter 5

1 Accenture (2018) How the U.S. wireless industry can drive future economic value [online] https://www.accenture.com/us-en/insights/strategy/wireless-industry-us-economy (archived at https://perma.cc/AN4Z-AXLF)

2 Accenture (nd) The race to the smart home, p. 10 [online] https://www.accenture.com/_acnmedia/pdf-50/accenture-race-to-the-smart-home.pdf (archived at https://perma.cc/Z7ZK-BGCB)

3 Whittaker, J (2018) Judge orders Amazon to turn over Echo recordings in double murder case, *Techcrunch* [online] https://techcrunch.com/2018/11/14/amazon-echo-recordings-judge-murder-case/ (archived at https://perma.cc/W7P6-5976)

4 Harvard Law Review (2018) Cooperation or resistance?: The role of tech companies in government surveillance [online] https://harvardlawreview.org/2018/04/cooperation-or-resistance-the-role-of-tech-companies-in-government-surveillance/ (archived at https://perma.cc/T3G8-ZN3V)

5 Whittaker, Z (2018) Amazon turns over record amount of customer data to US law enforcement, *ZDNet* [online] https://www.zdnet.com/article/amazon-turns-over-record-amount-of-customer-data-to-us-law-enforcement/ (archived at https://perma.cc/2MDN-X4BJ)

6 Accenture (2017) Cost of cyber crime study [online] https://www.
accenture.com/t20170926t072837z__w__/us-en/_acnmedia/pdf-61/
accenture-2017-costcybercrimestudy.pdf (archived at https://perma.cc/
Y88J-FRK3)

7 Pascu, L (2019) Millennials least likely to trust smart devices, Accenture
finds, *Bitdefender* [online] https://www.bitdefender.com/box/blog/smart-
home/millennials-least-likely-trust-smart-devices-accenture-finds/ (archived
at https://perma.cc/KX2B-2XF4)

8 Accenture (nd) Securing the digital economy [online] https://www.
accenture.com/se-en/insights/cybersecurity/_acnmedia/thought-leadership-
assets/pdf/accenture-securing-the-digital-economy-reinventing-the-internet-
for-trust.pdf#zoom=50 (archived at https://perma.cc/WWY7-VLVU)

9 Accenture (2018) Building pervasive cyber resilience now [online]
https://www.accenture.com/_acnmedia/pdf-81/accenture-build-pervasive-
cyber-resilience-now-landscape.pdf#zoom=50 (archived at
https://perma.cc/5X68-A8RJ)

10 Ibid

11 Accenture (nd) Digital trust in the IoT era [online] https://www.accenture.
com/_acnmedia/accenture/conversion-assets/dotcom/documents/global/pdf/
dualpub_18/accenture-digital-trust.pdf#zoom=50 (archived at
https://perma.cc/W4HV-2AVS)

12 Accenture (2018) Gaining ground on the cyber attacker: 2018 state of
cyber resilience [online] https://www.accenture.com/_acnmedia/pdf-76/
accenture-2018-state-of-cyber-resilience.pdf#zoom=50 (archived at
https://perma.cc/3AVB-PH73)

13 Wi-Fi Alliance (nd) Certification [online] https://www.wi-fi.org/certification
(archived at https://perma.cc/6ZZN-BHFZ)

14 Perkins Coie (1029) Regulating the security of connected devices: Are you
ready? [online] https://www.perkinscoie.com/en/news-insights/regulating-
the-security-of-connected-devices-are-you-ready.html (archived at
https://perma.cc/6B3C-HKUU)

15 Accenture (nd) Ready, set, smart: CSPs and the race to the smart home
[online] https://www.accenture.com/se-en/smart-home (archived at
https://perma.cc/KA9C-W2JZ)

16 Accenture (nd) The race to the smart home: why communications service
providers must defend and grow this critical market, p. 6 [online]
https://www.accenture.com/_acnmedia/pdf-50/accenture-race-to-the-smart-
home.pdf (archived at https://perma.cc/Z7ZK-BGCB)

17 Accenture (nd) The race to the smart home: Why Communications Service Providers must defend and grow this critical market [online] https://www. accenture.com/_acnmedia/pdf-50/accenture-race-to-the-smart-home.pdf (archived at https://perma.cc/8JV8-LHAF)

18 Accenture (nd) Securing the digital economy [online] https://www. accenture.com/_acnmedia/thought-leadership-assets/pdf/accenture-securing-the-digital-economy-reinventing-the-internet-for-trust.pdf (archived at https://perma.cc/P7E8-3VNK)

Chapter 6

1 Gleeson, D (2019) Smart home devices and services forecast: 2018–2023, Ovum [online] https://ovum.informa.com/resources/product-content/smart-home-devices-and-services-forecast-201823-ces004-000076 (archived at https://perma.cc/G8RM-W736)

2 Accenture (2019) Reshape to Relevance: 2019 Digital Consumer Survey, p. 2 [online] https://www.accenture.com/_acnmedia/pdf-93/accenture-digital-consumer-2019-reshape-to-relevance.pdf (archived at https://perma.cc/7GUJ-GZ3F)

3 Accenture (nd) The race to the smart home: why communications service providers must defend and grow this critical market, p. 9 [online] https://www.accenture.com/_acnmedia/pdf-50/accenture-race-to-the-smart-home.pdf (archived at https://perma.cc/Z7ZK-BGCB)

4 Accenture (2018) Accenture to help Swisscom enhance its customer experience [online] https://newsroom.accenture.com/news/accenture-to-help-swisscom-enhance-its-customer-experience.htm (archived at https://perma.cc/S89N-DSZQ)

5 Wilson, C (2017) CenturyLink using AI to boost sales efficiency, Light Reading [online] http://www.lightreading.com/automation/centurylink-using-ai-to-boost-sales-efficiency/d/d-id/735575 (archived at https://perma.cc/87XG-TRQD)

6 Cramshaw, J (nd) AI in telecom operations: opportunities & obstacles, *Guavus* [online] https://www.guavus.com/wp-content/uploads/2018/10/AI-in-Telecom-Operations_Opportunities_Obstacles.pdf (archived at https://perma.cc/5G98-PAC4); Hopwell, J (2018) Mobile World Congress: Telefonica launches Aura, announces Movistar Home, *Variety* [online] https://variety.com/2018/digital/global/mobile-world-congress-telefonica-aura-movistar-home-1202710220/ (archived at https://perma.cc/VX6G-MBNE)

7 Accenture (nd) Intelligent automation at scale : what's the hold up? p. 5 [online] https://www.accenture.com/_acnmedia/pdf-100/accenture-automation-at-scale-pov.pdf (archived at https://perma.cc/N23G-E2Q2)

8 Accenture (nd) Future ready: intelligent technology meets human ingenuity to create the future telco workforce, p. 8 [online] https://www.accenture.com/_acnmedia/pdf-93/accenture-5064a-future-ready-ai-pov-web.pdf#zoom=50 (archived at https://perma.cc/5KU2-4MVC)

9 For more background on the Pervasive Network see here: https://www.accenture.com/_acnmedia/pdf-81/accenture-network-capturing-promise-pervasive-pov-june-2018.pdf#zoom=50 (archived at https://perma.cc/X7ZH-DML4)

Chapter 7

1 Weidenbrück, M (2017) Hello Magenta! With Smart Speaker, your home listens to your command, *Telekom* [online] https://www.telekom.com/en/media/media-information/consumer-products/with-smart-speaker-your-home-listens-to-your-command-508276 (archived at https://perma.cc/959R-2BN2); Orange (2019) Orange launches the voice assistant Djingo to make its customers' everyday lives easier [online] https://www.orange.com/en/Press-Room/press-releases/press-releases-2019/Orange-launches-the-voice-assistant-Djingo-to-make-its-customers-everyday-lives-easier (archived at https://perma.cc/DJX6-QGR4); Morris, I (2018) Djingo Unchained: Orange, DT take AI fight to US tech giants, *Light Reading* [online] https://www.lightreading.com/artificial-intelligence-machine-learning/djingo-unchained-orange-dt-take-ai-fight-to-us-tech-giants/d/d-id/748249 (archived at https://perma.cc/3KC7-JJN8)

2 Japan Times (2019) NTT Docomo to discontinue decades-old i-mode, world's first mobile internet service, in 2026 [online] https://www.japantimes.co.jp/news/2019/10/29/business/tech/ntt-docomo-discontinue-decades-old-mode-worlds-first-mobile-internet-service-2026/#.Xe0KfzNKg2w (archived at https://perma.cc/KUU9-B7WP); bnamericas (2017) Analysis: Why is Telefônica shutting down Terra? [online] https://www.bnamericas.com/en/news/analysis-why-is-telefonica-shutting-down-terra (archived at https://perma.cc/8P37-G7DD); *manager magazin* (2015) Ströer kauft T-Online, Telekom wird Großaktionär [online] https://www.manager-magazin.de/digitales/it/stroeer-kauft-t-online-a-1047997.html (archived at https://perma.cc/4FT6-2REB)

3 Lee, J (2019) Celebrating 100,000 Alexa Skills –100,000 thank yous to you, *Amazon* [online] https://developer.amazon.com/blogs/alexa/post/c2d062ff-17b3-47f6-b256-f12c7e20f594/congratulations-alexa-skill-builders-100-000-skills-and-counting (archived at https://perma.cc/YAR2-45XP); Kinsella, B (2018) Amazon now has more than 50,000 Alexa Skills in the U.S. and it has tripled the rate of new skills added per day, *voicebot.ai* [online] https://voicebot.ai/2018/11/23/amazon-now-has-more-than-50000-alexa-skills-in-the-u-s-and-it-has-tripled-the-rate-of-new-skills-added-per-day/ (archived at https://perma.cc/5NVC-LKX9)

4 Accenture (2018) Accenture to help Swisscom enhance its customer experience [online] https://newsroom.accenture.com/news/accenture-to-help-swisscom-enhance-its-customer-experience.htm (archived at https://perma.cc/S89N-DSZQ)

5 Telia (nd) Smart Family [online] https://www.telia.fi/kauppa/kodin-netti/smart-family (archived at https://perma.cc/BTP5-2KC7)

6 Dayaratna, A (2018) IDC's Worldwide Developer Census, 2018: Part-time developers lead the expansion of the global developer population, IDC [online] https://www.idc.com/getdoc.jsp?containerId=US44363318 (archived at https://perma.cc/G45A-7PB4)

7 Herscovici, D (2017) Comcast closes Icontrol acquisition and plans to create a center of excellence for Xfinity Home, *Comcast* [online] https://corporate.comcast.com/comcast-voices/comcast-closes-icontrol-acquisition (archived at https://perma.cc/33RM-ETVR); Qivicon [online] https://www.qivicon.com/en/ (archived at https://perma.cc/H6E9-GUW6)

Chapter 8

1 Eclipse (2018) Smart Home Day @Eclipsecon Europe 2018 [online] https://www.eclipse.org/smarthome/blog/2018/10/29/smarthomeday.html (archived at https://perma.cc/LJR6-YLGC)

2 Schüßler, A (2020) LinkedIn post [online] https://www.linkedin.com/posts/axel-schuessler-17406182_iot-developers-openhab-activity-6620611740122046464-bW4n/ (archived at https://perma.cc/8J9U-TZH3)

3 Das, S (2016) IoT standardization: problem of plenty? *CIO&Leader* [online] https://www.cioandleader.com/article/2016/02/09/iot-standardization-problem-plenty (archived at https://perma.cc/352C-HM6X)

4 Web of Things working group [online] https://www.w3.org/WoT/WG/ (archived at https://perma.cc/24HE-7WCU)

5 Ibid

6 Ibid

Chapter 9

1 Long, J, Roark, C and Theofilou, B (2018) The Bottom Line on Trust, Accenture [online] https://www.accenture.com/us-en/insights/strategy/trust-in-business (archived at https://perma.cc/D57X-RUXU)

INDEX